D1522797

Creative Revolt

American University Studies

Series XXIV
American Literature

Vol. 12

PETER LANG
New York • Bern • Frankfurt am Main • Paris

Michael F. Lynch

Creative Revolt

A Study of Wright,
Ellison, and Dostoevsky

PETER LANG
New York • Bern • Frankfurt am Main • Paris

Library of Congress Cataloging-in-Publication Data

Lynch, Michael F.
   Creative revolt : a study of Wright, Ellison, and
Dostoevsky / Michael F. Lynch.
      p. cm. — (American university studies. Series
XXIV. American literature ; vol. 12)
      Bibliography: p.
      Includes index.
      1. American fiction—Afro-American authors—
History and criticism.   2. American fiction—20th century—
History and criticism.   3. Wright, Richard, 1906-1960—
Criticism and interpretation.   4. Ellison, Ralph—
Criticism and interpretation.   5. Dostoyevsky, Fyodor,
1821-1881—Influence.   6. Literature, Comparative—
American and Russian.   7. Literature, Comparative—
Russian and American.   8. American fiction—Russian
influences.   9. Afro-Americans in literature.
10. Existentialism in literature.   I. Title   II. Series.
PS153.N5L96   1990   810.9'896—dc20   89-32225
ISBN 0-8204-1018-7   CIP
ISSN 0895-0512

CIP-Titelaufnahme der Deutschen Bibliothek

Lynch, Michael F.:
Creative revolt : a study of Wright, Ellison, and
Dostoevsky / Michael F. Lynch. — New York;
Bern; Frankfurt am Main; Paris: Lang, 1990.
   (American University Studies: Ser. 24,
   American Literature; Vol. 12)
   ISBN 0-8204-1018-7

NE: American University Studies / 24

ₒ Publishing, Inc., New York 1990

Printed by Weihert-Druck GmbH, Darmstadt, West Germany

for my parents

Joseph and Hannah Lynch

Contents

Contents

Introduction

> This past, the Negro's past, of rope, fire, torture, this past, this
> endless struggle to achieve and reveal and confirm a human
> identity, human authority, yet contains, for all its horror, some-
> thing very beautiful. I do not mean to be sentimental about
> suffering--enough is as good as a feast--but people who cannot
> suffer can never grow up, can never discover who they are.
> (Baldwin, *Fire* 113)

These words of James Baldwin suggest one of the most basic similarities
between the world-view of the nineteenth-century Russian masters of fiction,
including Dostoevsky, and that of the leading writers of mid-twentieth-century
black American fiction, Richard Wright and Ralph Ellison. The experience of
the redemptive and even sacramental character of suffering which inspired
nineteenth-century Russians has also sustained black Americans through their
long watch for the conversion of white America to a thorough self-knowledge
and a proper self-love which would no longer feel the need for violence,
discrimination, or hatred. As Baldwin indicates, this attitude toward suffering
mysteriously nurtures a loving and healing force, especially in the heart of the
sufferer or the oppressed:

> Love is a battle, love is a war, love is a growing up. No one in the
> world knows more, knows Americans better or, odd as this may
> sound, loves them more than the American Negro. This is because
> he has had to watch you, outwit you, deal with you, and bear you,
> and sometimes even bleed and die with you, ever since we got
> here, that is, since both of us, black and white, got here--and this
> is a wedding. (*Nobody* 136)

Both nineteenth-century Russian writers and twentieth-century black

American writers have tended to see themselves not as cursed by their tribulations but rather as set apart and invested with the special mission of helping to save others, even those who most directly cause their suffering. The messianic consciousness of Russia as a "God-bearing people" called by God to save the West permeates Russian fiction throughout the nineteenth century. Nikolai Gogol describes this "supreme triumph of spiritual solidity" as

> something more than ordinary love for the fatherland. Why are neither France nor England nor Germany infested by this fad, why do they not prophesy about themselves, why is Russia the only one to prophesy? Because more strongly than the others does it feel the hand of God in all which has been visited upon her, and it scents the approach of a new kingdom. (*Passages* 51)

Though black American writers have been generally less explicit in their investigations of messianic and apocalyptic themes, they share in general a commitment to prophetic utterance, as well as to a search for moral and spiritual values which parallels the Russians' efforts to transform their "superfluous men" into useful and dynamic individuals. Jean Toomer's *Cane* (1925) might be compared to Pushkin's *Eugene Onegin* (1831) as one of the finest achievements of a newly mature literature and as an expression of deep yearning for artists and leaders who would be intellectually and morally responsible. In somewhat the same way that nineteenth-century Russians saw their destiny as interwoven with that of the West, black fiction has often implied that the fate of America will be decided by the fate of black Americans, depending on how blacks respond to their suffering and on whether white Americans will grow enough to appreciate and love this integral part of their own culture. As Baldwin puts it, the black is "the key figure in his country, and the American future is precisely as bright or as dark as his" (*Fire* 108).

Aside from a spiritual and transcendent attitude toward suffering, a central theme of both literatures is the struggle with the dialectic of personality-versus-society, of the dignity and freedom of the individual versus collectivist, materialist, and authoritarian movements for social reorganization. Many Russian writers of the period from the 1820s and Pushkin through the formulation of the principles of socialist realism after the 1917 revolution, contributed to the intense search for a means of reconciling the value of individual freedom with the hope for a more compassionate and humane society. Of the many who wrestled with the dialectic, however, not all came to recognize its root contradiction: that any materialistic and/or authoritarian social movement, no matter how well motivated by earnest compassion to provide greater freedom for people, necessarily sets itself against individual freedom and inevitably opposes human subjectivity, creativity, and dignity. The social and literary critics Alexander Herzen and Vissarion Belinsky, philosophers Vladimir Solovyov and Nikolai Berdyaev, and Dostoevsky figure among the Russian intellectuals whose exploration of this problem resulted in their vigorous defense of the primacy of the individual, and in their critique of any system of thought or political movement which does not subscribe to this primary value. Both Berdyaev and Dostoevsky made youthful and seemingly tentative commitments to forms of radical and materialistic socialism; but both repudiated their belief in collectivism and spent virtually their entire careers in the service of the human personality.

The "solution" of the dialectic of personality-versus-society typically found in nineteenth-century Russian fiction, and especially in Dostoevsky, consists of an analysis of the roles of conscience and responsibility in the individual who freely surrenders his revolt through a new love of community. Perhaps because Dostoevsky himself at one point devoted some allegiance to a form of collectivism, he masterfully presents both sides of the problem--not always fairly, but with consistent passion and brilliance. Berdyaev, for a brief time a proponent of Marxism, criticized it along with Russian atheism as "a dialectical moment in the development of the Russian soul and Russian consciousness" (*Idea* 252). He found communism "a distortion of the Russian messianic idea," its truth "the spirit of brotherhood and its falsehood the narrowing of personality" (*Idea* 250). The "dialectical moment" of which Berdyaev speaks, as well as the attempt to depict both sides of the issue, can be observed also in the fiction of Richard Wright and Ralph Ellison. Both Wright and Ellison underwent a period of dedication to collectivism in the form of the Communist Party in America before rejecting authoritarian materialism for essentially the same reason which motivated Dostoevsky. Like the fiction of Dostoevsky, their work, especially Wright's *Native Son, The Outsider,* and "The Man Who Lived Underground," as well as Ellison's *Invisible Man*, refutes the claims of determinism and materialistic collectivism and posits instead the mystery and value of the human personality. Both Wright and Ellison admired and were greatly influenced by Dostoevsky. Only a few articles have suggested some of the connections between Wright and Dostoevsky, and no extended study has been done in this area.

The struggle of the individual to realize and test his freedom could be named as the theme most common to Dostoevsky, Wright, and Ellison. Dostoevsky and Ellison see unlimited self-assertion as resulting in loss of personality and in the weakening of life-giving communal bonds. Although Wright offers two major protagonists whose self-will harms themselves and the community, he colors their tragedies with strong tones of respect and admiration for their growth in self-knowledge and freedom. While Dostoevsky and Ellison assert the individual's need to limit self-will and to make a creative social contribution, Wright in *Native Son* and The Outsider gives freer rein and qualified approval to the explorer of "absolute" freedom, even if this freedom involves the violation of others' most basic rights.

Dostoevsky's split from radical socialist thinking after his arrest and penal term in Siberia signaled the end of his possible dalliance with materialism. His refutations of materialistic determinism, collectivism, and atheism resound with cumulative power through *The House of the Dead, Notes from Underground, Crime and Punishment, The Idiot, The Devils*, and *The Brothers Karamazov. The House of the Dead* presents evidence that the convict in the harshest, most controlled prison environment will assert his freedom of personality even when such action worsens his situation. *Notes from Underground* extends such observations to the universal level. Dostoevsky argues that man cannot and will not accept a rational utopia based on one's own advantage because free will or self-assertion remains psychologically man's most precious "possession" or capacity, even when it causes one harm or self-destruction. *Crime and Punishment* portrays the first of Dostoevsky's protagonists including Raskolnikov, Stavrogin, Kirilov, and Ivan Karamazov, whose revolt seems to justify and even require the suspension of all morality--much like the cases of Wright's Bigger Thomas, Cross Damon, and Fred Daniels, as well as Ellison's Invisible Man. Yet Raskolnikov's disastrous experiment in anti-metaphysics only demonstrates that he *lacks* the right to take human life at will. Prince Myshkin of *The Idiot* symbolizes and embodies loving selflessness, but his Christian dedication and sacrifice cannot transform or save a world ruled by greed and self-absorption. With Stavrogin, Kirilov, and Shatov of *The Devils* Dostoevsky develops parallel cases of three men who survive extremes of self-will, reject authoritarian collectivism for its denigration of human freedom, and find a mystical or moral awakening in self-surrender.

Through all the major novels Dostoevsky shows modern man's penchant and deep need for revolt caused by the dominant forces of egoism and the apparent disappearance of God. He demonstrates that the passionate thinker or seeker in the modern age often must pass through some profound form of negation first (e.g., nihilism, amoralism, atheism) before he can achieve integration or sanctity or happiness. *The Brothers Karamazov* especially stresses self-assertion as a virtually necessary stage in the individual's development. It also amplifies Dostoevsky's theme of freedom not just as a right or a fact of man's psychology, but as his greatest challenge. Wright and Ellison also stress this modern need for revolt, but Wright in *Native Son* and *The Outsider* does not depict any way *back from*, or beyond nihilistic rebellion, at times glamorizing to some extent its creative, heroic, and existential aspects. Ellison, on the other hand, suggests as does Dostoevsky the sterility and futility of egoistic assertion which does not discover its dialectical fulfillment in love for others.

Both Wright and Ellison were reared in the school of American literary naturalism featuring Stephen Crane, Frank Norris, and Theodore Dreiser, with its strong deterministic emphasis on environment; and their early stories minimize the power of the individual to effect social change. They heeded the call of the political radicals of the 1930s for freedom and for changes in the basic structure of American society. As their careers developed, their demand for freedom remained militant in a sense, but proceeded inward. Both writers evidently were influenced by Dostoevsky's insights not just on the necessity for freedom of personality, but also on the risks and potentially crushing burden of that freedom.

The naturalist tinge of defeatism is stronger in Wright's early work than in Ellison's, though in *Uncle Tom's Children* the oppressed blacks derive some hope through glimmerings of collective political action. The emphasis on environment dominates *Native Son*, despite its awkward and somewhat confusing admixture of existentialism. Bigger Thomas, having accidentally sundered the fetters of his existence through a killing, acquires a sense of self and freedom more meaningful to him than the lives of others. *The Outsider* clarifies Wright's rejection of communism and naturalism with his profound existential statement of modern man's duty to recognize and act upon his freedom. Taking Bigger's revolt several steps further, Cross Damon slips through the bars of his environment and finds nothing to restrain him from killing at will, until he wishes belatedly to love a woman and start a new life. While Wright notes the tragic and even demonic nature of such unbridled self-assertion, he regrets, as does Ivan Karamazov, that the absence of God opens up abominable possibilities of despair. Ellison's early stories and essays, despite their radical and communist sympathies, betray a deeper interest than Wright's in black folklore and tradition--and a non-defeatist attitude--which soon turned him away from naturalism and toward his eventual creed of fluidity and possibility. Like the work of Dostoevsky and Wright, *Invisible Man* shows the individual's need for creative rebellion in order to choose and define himself over against dehumanizing social structures and organizations. Ellison strikes a more optimistic chord than Wright does generally, seeing the limits of one's self-assertion as an invitation to meaningful social connection.

All three writers, therefore, are united by their growth in disaffection with materialistic explanations of human behavior and with radical, collectivist political activity. All three offer evidence of human freedom as an irrepressible facet of existence; they also caution the individual against too selfish or solipsistic a program of self-assertion, believing that freedom entails responsibility to oneself and to others. Wright stresses the power of conscience and responsibility to others to a lesser degree in *Native Son* and *The Outsider*, where his protagonists feel no remorse for their murders. To an extent, then, he reverses Dostoevsky's thesis of the murderer driven by guilt toward the surrender of self-will. Wright shows that both Bigger and Cross need to exercise real responsibility and thus become more than superfluous men for whom society provides neither a place nor a means of making their creative contributions. In these two works, however, Wright places the individual's responsibility to assert self and freedom above his social responsibility, resulting in an existential outlook which at times tends to glorify self-will. "The Man Who Lived Underground" establishes more of a positive ideal with Fred Daniels who, very similar to Dmitry Karamazov, discovers his desire to be connected with all other people and finds joy in giving up his ultimate but rootless and meaningless freedom. Ellison acknowledges his debt to this story and to Dostoevsky in *Invisible Man*, where he, too, explores the need for individual revolt and for the transcendence of self-will.

This study analyzes the parallel development of Dostoevsky, Wright, and Ellison away from naturalism and collectivism and toward existential freedom.

It also focuses on Dostoevsky's evident influence on Wright and Ellison and on their adaptations of and responses to certain of his observations and themes. Chapter One treats Dostoevsky's early socialism and his sympathy with determinism and subsequent reaction against it. Chapter Two discusses Wright's and Ellison's conscious debt to Dostoevsky, as well as their early involvement with communism and their defection from it. Chapter Three presents *Native Son* and *The Outsider* as written largely in the shadow of *Crime and Punishment,* but as vacillating somewhat between endorsing complete self-assertion and recognizing its potential for self-destruction. Chapter Four develops all three writers' criticisms of determinism, materialism, and collectivism by focusing on their analyses of freedom and their shared ideal of social responsibility as found in *The Devils, The Brothers Karamazov,* "The Man Who Lived Underground," and *Invisible Man.*

Chapter 1

Dostoevsky's Early Socialism and Reaction against Determinism

I

Dostoevsky, Wright, and Ellison each made a commitment in his youth to a radical socialist or communist group; but before long each one began to see that the authoritarian and materialist nature of the group actually contravened its professed value of human freedom and the dignity of the individual. Consequently, in the early work of each writer one finds a subtle irresolution in the implied belief in environment which leads gradually to a refutation of collectivism and materialism; and this refutation becomes a sustaining theme through most of each writer's mature work. This chapter and the next will examine first Dostoevsky's and then Wright's and Ellison's radical involvement and later disenchantment, and will also discuss their early fiction reflecting either vacillation toward or outright rejection of materialism and the collectivist ideal.

Dostoevsky's membership in the radical Petrashevsky circle remains somewhat obscure, but evidence indicates that he had made a serious, if ill-advised commitment to the group before his arrest and sentence to hard labor and exile in Siberia. His two major works before exile, *Poor Folk* and *The Double*, show him vacillating between personal responsibility and environment as the primary contributor to human suffering. His first major works after exile, *The House of the Dead, Winter Notes on Summer Impressions*, and *Notes from Underground*, comprise the first draft of his mature criticism of determinism and rationalist materialism, the opening salvo of his personal war on those ideologies that would carry him through virtually all his subsequent work. Wright's eight-year formal membership in the Communist Party represents the strongest radical tie of the three writers. But even in *Lawd Today*, his first novel (unpublished until after his death) and in *Uncle Tom's Children*, a sequence of short stories and his first major published work, one can detect doubts about collective action and vacillation between communist ideology and more deeply rooted black nationalistic sympathies. Ellison's course in radicalism paralleled but did not reach the intensity of Wright's, leading Ellison to sympathy and alignment with, but not membership in the Party. Ellison's doubts are implied in his stories and essays earlier and with more definition than are Wright's, surfacing in his emphasis on black folklore and in his tiring of the bleakness and defeat in much naturalistic fiction.

In order to discuss Dostoevsky's involvement with radical socialism, and in order to become acquainted with some of the issues which affected Wright and Ellison as well, a sketch of early Russian socialism and radicalism is first necessary. The critic Belinsky, in his famous "Letter to Gogol," a castigation of Gogol's apparent abandonment of social criticism in *Select Passages from Correspondence with Friends*, attacked Gogol for his failure to assert the highest value of nineteenth-century Russian writers, namely human dignity:

> You failed to see that Russia sees her salvation not in mysticism
> or asceticism or pietism, but in the successes of civilization,
> enlightenment, and humanity. What she needs is not sermons or
> prayers, but the awakening in the people of a sense of their human
> dignity lost for so many centuries amid dirt and refuse. (84)

Belinsky's statement illustrates the centrality of concern for the individual among both the conservative and radical Russian intelligentsia. In fact, as Wayne Dowler points out, throughout most of the century both conservatives and radicals sought as a primary goal the freedom of the personality and the moral salvation of the individual (9). Dowler adds that "both camps feared the egoism and acquisitiveness and the specialization and mechanism that they identified with Western bourgeois society. They wished to preserve the free activity of the integrated personality as the prime creative force in society and culture" (94).

Some early socialists, most notably Belinsky, were strongly influenced by Hegel's philosophy, which contained clear implications of the inevitability of social progress but which was also rigidly anti-personalist. For Hegel, the individual's submission to the "objective" facts of existence and his acceptance of the status quo, especially absolute monarchy, constituted the highest form of the "rational" (Malia 204). Hegel saw his idea as a paradox: "Thus the individual personality, by losing itself in science does not irretrievably perish. The personality must repudiate itself in order to become the vessel of truth. . . . To die to natural immediacy means to be resurrected in the spirit" (Malia 248). But, though not entirely materialistic, Hegel's position amounted to the destruction of the free personality pursuing its unique goals (Dowler 51). Belinsky's reading of Hegel in the late 1830s resulted in his short period of conservatism, to which his friend Alexander Herzen, one of the few Russian socialists at the time, reacted with anger. Herzen's influence cured Belinsky of his previous disdain for political and social concerns and of his temporary endorsement of Hegelian anti-personalism. It also helped make Belinsky a strong adherent of the new French social doctrines (Frank 122). In 1840, after Belinsky's graduation from Hegelianism, he became a revolutionary overnight (Mathewson 5).

Many other socialists were better equipped to resist the temptations of Hegelianism by their solid foundations in personalist philosophy and litera-ture. The German philosopher Schelling agreed with Hegel's idea of history as a sequential revelation of God, but he rejected Hegel's tenet that revelation was accomplished through external compulsion. For Hegel, the personality of individuals was subsumed in the impersonal World Spirit; Schelling held the contrary view, that life exists only in the unique potentiality of individuals (Dowler 51). German idealism, whose influence in Russia succeeded that of French classicism and rationalism in the 1820's, molded Herzen and much of his generation while it inaugurated a revolution in the philosophical tradition of Europe (Malia 72). According to Martin Malia, German idealism tended to foster egocentrism, but underscored personalism and somehow inspired the individual to look beyond himself for fulfillment:

> The salient characteristic of idealism is an unbounded egocen-
> trism. God, the Absolute, nature, and the whole of world history
> come to focus in the self. . . . Idealism's strong affirmation of the
> individual's selfhood is matched by an equally strong yearning to
> belong, to participate meaningfully in collectivities which tran-
> scend the self. (77)

Some conservative romantics, such as the Germans Novalis and Muller, subordinated the individual to the unity of the community, but these were in the minority (Dowler 19). Schiller, perhaps the most influential German romantic for Herzen's and Dostoevsky's generation, sought the self-fulfillment of the individual in the world of beauty. But while he too promoted personalism over rationalism and materialism, the implications of his thought left the individual stranded in a state of permanent adolescence, egoism, and self-pity (Malia 43).

Although several men were involved in the birth of Russian socialism, Herzen generally is credited as its author as well as its most interesting and articulate promoter. Herzen stood as an enemy of abstraction and Hegelian anti-personalism and as a faithful and stalwart spokesman for the freedom of the individual, especially (if ironically) after Herzen's conversion to a form of positivism or materialism early in his socialist career. This "gentry revolution-ary" together with his friend Nikolai Ogaryov provided Russia's only link between the failed Decembrist uprising in 1825 and the growing agitation in the following years for democratization and reform. The failed European revolutions of 1830 convinced Herzen that the true liberation of Europe called for a social and not just a political revolution (Malia 104). Socialism as it was evolving in Russia in the 1830s did not yet mean the abolition of all private property, but it did aim at a collectivization of wealth and at economic as opposed to purely political reform. As Malia explains,

> Its emphasis on the ''collective'' was simply an insistence that *all* men must have the right to become complete human beings. Reform must be universal in order to give each and every individual a decent, humane life and freedom for the full development of his personality, since the emancipation of no man is complete without the emancipation of all men. . . . By 1840, as frustration and repression continued, the term socialism came into general use to denote any doctrine that viewed reform as the total transformation of society and not just of certain institutions. Shortly thereafter the word communism became current to signify more precisely the radical equalizing of wealth. (114)

Herzen's socialism always focused on the themes of individual liberty and freedom of speech rather than on social or economic equality. In the early forties he was quite sympathetic to religious socialism, admiring Christianity as an incarnation of the idea of the sanctity of the individual (Malia 306). In *From the Other Shore* he stated that "socialism corresponds to the Nazarene teaching in the Roman Empire" (89). Yet he criticized the "Christian-feudal" affirmation of individuality as an alienated one since the Christian promise of equality supposedly remained only a promise throughout this life (Malia 315). In the mid-forties, however, Herzen's ideas underwent a transformation from the idealism and religious interest of his youth to a form of positivism and materialism. Having concluded that all ideas, including religion, were simply emanations of man's nervous system, he rejected not idealist metaphysics as such but all revealed religion in favor of rationalism (Malia 182), which, ironically, was precisely what he had rebelled against and would continue to reject in Hegel. Herzen's rather contradictory attitude toward idealism, as well as his inconsistent devotion both to materialism and to the dignity or "sanctity" of the individual personality, might be seen as a prototype of the inconsistency that would affect Dostoevsky, Wright, and Ellison in the early stages of their careers.

Through the late forties Herzen's pioneering socialism was eclipsed by the movement's wider dissemination, but his insistence on the primacy of the personality in the dialectic with community remained as his most important legacy. With the appearance in 1845 of the Petrashevsky circle, the first large socialist group and the one to which Dostoevsky would belong, Herzen's socialism was no longer a phenomenon of such high visibility. His optimum socialism would make individuality and community harmonious rather than antithetical principles; his ideal consisted of their reconciliation in an *obschina* or peasant commune which would preserve democratic equality (Malia 325). As Herzen's words illustrate, he feared that communal organization might swallow up the individual: "To keep the commune and give freedom to the individual, to spread that self-government now existing in the villages and the districts to the cities and to the whole country, while at the same time preserving national unity--in this consists the question of the future of Russia'' (Malia 405). Perhaps as a defense for the individual, and in the tradition of some German idealists such as Schiller, Herzen's ideal of personality tended toward egoism and a self-consciousness which assumed the right to create its own morality (as do many of the protagonists of Dostoevsky, Wright, and Ellison). In *From the Other Shore* Herzen rejected all system-building and authoritarianism, accepting only a humanism which recognizes the person as an end in himself. He surrendered his cherished belief in progress as a corollary of Hegel's "slaughter-bench of history," the idea which held that the individual exists merely to advance some ''objective'' law to an ideal future.

In the balance, then, Herzen's stolid assertion of human freedom may be viewed as an early form of existentialism, somewhat parallel to that of his contemporary Kierkegaard. Malia notes that "Herzen's socialism was collectivistic in form but individualistic in content. It should be clear that the latter trait was distinctly the more important of the two" (421). Ironically, Herzen, the leading figure of early Russian socialism, was, according to Isaiah Berlin, "perhaps the most devastating opponent of the many Communisms of his day, who declared that no ideal at which one was forbidden to smile was worth anything at all" (xxi). As Herzen himself summed up his position, "For months I have been calculating and pondering and vacillating, and have finally sacrificed everything to: Human Dignity and Free Speech. . . . The liberty of the individual is the greatest thing of all; it is on this and this alone that the true will of the people can develop" (12). His clear rejection of the implications of determinism places Herzen in the company of the mature Dostoevsky, Wright, and Ellison: "Man is a great deal freer than is usually believed. He depends a great deal on his environment, but not so much as he surrenders to it. A large part of our destiny lies in our hands" (127). Malia universalizes the problem with which these men struggled: "The modern history of all countries, and in particular of Russia, demonstrates that the practical problem of combining individual liberty with revolutionary democratization is one of immense difficulty and that both ideals inevitably become tarnished in their application" (425).

The first and second generations of Russian radical theorists, led by Belinsky in the forties and then Chernyshevsky, Dobrolyubov, and Pisarev in the fifties and sixties, although profoundly affected by Herzen's socialism, effectively broke with his personalism (though perhaps not always consciously) and pursued determinism and a narrower and more consistent materialism which ultimately laid the foundation for the twentieth-century doctrine of socialist realism. Rufus Mathewson's comment that "to discover consistency in Belinsky is to distort him" (25) is especially true of Belinsky in the mid-forties, when he was oscillating between a moral-religious humanism and a more "rational" materialism and determinism. Belinsky resolved this conflict, however, when he came to the conclusion that "in the words 'God' and 'religion' I see darkness, gloom, chains, and the knout, and now I like these two words as much as the four following them" (Frank 186). Frank sees these words as marking "the moment when atheism and socialism fused together in Russia into an alliance never afterwards to be completely dissolved" (186), although this alliance weakened for a time in the 1870s. Belinsky sharply criticized and essentially dismissed Dostoevsky's second novel, *The Double*, a brilliant examination of a person's decaying sense of self-worth and dignity. In this criticism can be seen Belinsky's eroding dedication to human dignity, or his failure to understand its more profound psychological aspects--an ironic development, in light of his later self-righteous attack on Gogol (in his "Letter to Gogol") for supposedly abandoning human dignity. Belinsky's new deterministic creed, together with his distraction with the externals of political and social issues, decidedly separates him from Herzen, for it seems to have robbed him of the fulfillment of his best intentions regarding the defense of human dignity.

Chernyshevsky, Dobrolyubov, and Pisarev, who were literary critics and the conscious heirs of Belinsky's radicalism in the next generation, typified the disgust of the men of the sixties for the "superfluous men" of the forties, whose high ideals and noble sentiments had culminated not in action or useful social change, but in mere *talk*. Dobrolyubov complained in an essay titled "When Will the Real Day Come?": "What has our society done during the past twenty or thirty years? So far, nothing. It studied, developed, listened to the Rudins, sympathized with them in their setbacks in the noble struggle for convictions, prepared for action, but it did not *do* anything" (119). Herzen, on the other hand, out of favor with the new young radicals, defended the dreamers of the previous generation, such as the "heroes" of Turgenev's *Rudin* and Goncharov's *Oblomov*, as honorable and pitiable victims of a hostile social system. Chernyshevsky, Dobrolyubov, and Pisarev, working in the tradition of Belinsky, sought to re-fashion the Russian concept of the hero along the lines of self-possession and confident, "useful" social action. One notices Dobrolyubov's determinist viewpoint in his pointing away from the defeated heroes of the past:

On the one hand, we have the utterly somnolent Oblomovs who have entirely lost even the charm of eloquence with which they enchanted young ladies in the past; on the other, we have the active Chichikovs who are unslumbering and tireless in their heroic pursuit of their narrow and sordid interests. . . . Where are the men of integrity who have been from childhood imbued with a single idea? There are no such men among us, because up to now our social environment has been unfavorable for their development. It is from this environment, from its banality and pettiness, that we must be liberated by the new men whose appearance is so impatiently and eagerly awaited by all that is best in our society. A little more vacillation, a few more powerful words and favorable factors, and active men will appear. (221, 225)

Chernyshevsky sounded a similar determinist note in his essay "The Russian at the Rendez-vous": "Everything depends on social customs and on circumstances. Look carefully, for what seems to be a person's fault may only be his misfortune. Guilt requires censure or even punishment. Misfortune calls for help to the individual by removing the circumstances that are stronger than his will" (105).

The minimization or denial of free will in these critics' determinist schema, which proceeded partly from Belinsky's rejection of or failure to understand personalism, undermined the vitality both of their concept of the hero and of their very literary aesthetic. Dobrolyubov's famous manifesto "What is Oblomovism?" was intended to prepare for the installation of the "new man," who would be abrupt, direct, fearless, practical, unsentimental, and selfless (Mathewson 99). Chernyshevsky's wooden novel *What Is to Be Done?* offers a supposedly exemplary man, Rakhmetov, a self-made superman and professional revolutionary who, as Mathewson says, "emerges finally as the monolithic personality Dobrolyubov sought in his criticism, with hardly an identifying mark of his humanity, or a single flaw to involve him in interesting, tension-producing situations" (77). In short, he is a bore. The debate over the aesthetics of radical art and protest (in which Wright and Ellison also have taken part) intensified in Russia in the 1860s largely because of the importation of

English Utilitarianism. Chernyshevsky shared Plato's disdain of art and treated it with an attitude of suspicious impatience (Mathewson 65). Pisarev, the most radical of these critics, in his essay "The Destruction of Aesthetics," held that a pair of shoes is better than a Shakespearean tragedy because shoes can be worn while nothing "useful" can come from a play (Matlaw, *Belinsky* xix). The sterile, anti-literary, thoroughly anti-personalist theory inherited from Belinsky and developed by these later radical critics thus ran *counter* to the initial, personalist socialism of Herzen, and began a tradition that would culminate in socialist realism. Mathewson exposes the rationale and the weakness of such protest:

> Radical art is virtually indifferent to universal statement. Because of the radicals' materialist distrust of absolutes and permanent categories, their kinds of social generalization do not readily extend themselves through time. Value is conferred on art from without, by the service it performs at any given moment, and, by all accounts, the modern Soviet reader is still expected to value *Dead Souls* for its expose of social conditions and to derive a kind of *ex post facto* indignation from it. (94)

As suggested above, the increasing influence of materialism and atheism on early socialism in Russia contributed to its gradually diminishing commitment to personalism. As the personalist commitment of socialism and radicalism proceeded to weaken in the sixties, the very idea of the spiritual quest for the dignity of the individual seemed an anachronism, an unfortunate holdover from the idle, self-conscious generation of superfluous men. Yet prior to the moment of the fusion of socialism and atheism in the mid-forties, many early Russian socialists were adopting or assimilating the principles of French *Christian* socialism, which carefully preserved the autonomy of the individual. The early Christian socialists saw their movement as an opportunity to "modernize" Christianity, to rectify the failings of many Christians in the past to apply concretely Christ's precepts of universal love and compassion. The apocalyptic or eschatological element of socialism, which survived long after its fusion with atheism, derived largely from the traditional Christian expectation and vision of a new world. Malia analyzes the Christian roots of much of the European agitation for social change which soon filtered down to Russia:

> Fourier, Pierre Leroux, Buches, Lammenais--in a word, almost all the social prophets of the thirties--not only believed in God, but considered that some form of religious cult was necessary to the complete man. They conceived of socialism as the final historical fulfillment of Christianity's original promise of universal brotherhood and love. . . . For the Saint-Simonians, early Christianity, the Reformation, the Enlightenment, 1789, and the future social revolution were successive and interrelated stages in the historical development of the ideas of the supreme worth of the individual and of human freedom. (118, 124)

Although a mild resurgence of Christian socialism took place in the 1870s, its early manifestation in the years 1830-48 differed significantly from early materialistic socialism because of its consistent "reverence for the sanctity of the individual that was, if anything, even greater than that of contemporary liberalism" (Malia 112). As will be seen below, Dostoevsky's early adherence to Christian socialism gave him a solid foundation in personalism which outlasted his brief but important relationship with radicalism.

The so-called "native soil" movement of the 1850s and early 1860s, led by Grigoryev and Dostoevsky, constituted a second wave of idealist reaction against the rising popularity of positivism. This movement offered the best hope for the individual with its program of reconciliation between the radicals and Westernizers on the one hand and the Slavophiles on the other (Dowler 29). Grigoryev, strongly antirationalist in elevating concrete, living experience over abstract theorizing, had praise and criticism both for those seeking the Europeanization of Russia and for those advocating Russia's reliance on her own strengths and religious traditions. The *pochvenniki*, or "men of the soil" in this movement, though fundamentally conservative, refused to view Peter's hurling Russia into European history either as the real inauguration of Russian history or as a break with the national character (Dowler 90). Seeking compromise, both Grigoryev and Dostoevsky held that although Westernism's support of the idea of progress focused on the elimination of individual differences, it squarely faced Russia's need for development. They recognized that Slavophilism and the Orthodox Church's doctrine of the primacy of conscience tended to strengthen the autonomy of the individual over that of the state (Malia 284). But the *pochvenniki* criticized the anti-personalist element both of Utilitarian Westernism and of Slavophilism. They objected to the former's theory of education, which stressed the student's learning practicality to the virtual exclusion of the human side of his character (Dowler 100). Dowler notes that the "men of the soil" sought to protect the individual:

> They were especially critical of the Slavophile view that education should aim at subsuming the individual personality in the immutable values of the community. Grigoryev complained as early as 1858 that "the idea of the annihilation of the individual in the communism of our Russian soul is precisely the weak side of Slavophilism." (99)

The native soil movement, true to its roots of idealism and personalist socialism in the previous generation, helped to preserve the value of the dignity and freedom of the individual through the particularly volatile fifties and sixties, embracing

> an educational theory based on individualism and freedom. They advocated neither severe social constraint nor revolutionary license. Rather, they placed their faith in the individual, in the moral worth of the autonomous personality.... Their rejection of state intervention to preserve, or revolutionary compulsion to transform society reflected their desire to secure the individual and society from the interference of reactionary authoritarian government on the one hand and from the ravages of revolutionary theory and practice on the other. (Dowler 105)

With the decline of the native soil movement after the death of its major promulgator Grigoryev in 1864, two of the few voices raised later in the century against materialist socialism and early Marxism belonged to the Christian philosophers Vladimir Solovyov and Nikolai Berdyaev. Solovyov, attempting to lead Russian thought out of the "temptations" of socialism, spoke of its "truth" as its rebellion against social evil; he saw it as justified historically, as the final step of the Western historical development that had preceded it. But in tracing the root of social untruth to egoism, he concluded that any socialism based on self-assertion (such as utilitarian socialism) contradicted itself and only contributed to social ill. Solovyov's insight regarding man's need for self-assertion before self-denial comes very close to (and may have been influenced by) that of Dostoevsky:

> If the root of social untruth consists of egoism, then social truth must be based upon the opposite of egoism, that is to say, upon the principle of self-denial or love for others. In order to realize that truth, every single member of society must set a limit to his exclusive self-assertion, must adopt the point of view of self-denial, must renounce his exclusive self-will, must sacrifice it. . . .
>
> The way toward brotherhood, toward the realization of true equality, true freedom and salvation, is that of self-denial. *For self-denial, however, a previous self-assertion is necessary.* (83, 87) (emphasis added)

Solovyov argued that the logical development of the principles of socialism and positivism leads, paradoxically and surprisingly, to "a demand for the religious principles in life and in knowledge" (86). He similarly turned the tables on materialism, accepting its basic tenets but deciding that "there are solid philosophical grounds for the assertion that the physical forces themselves can be reduced to the spiritual" (97).

Berdyaev was the final great spokesman in nineteenth-century Russia for the sanctity of the individual over, in this case, Marxism. Like Wright and Ellison much later, Berdyaev had a passion for social justice that led him to become a professed Marxist for some time, but he could never conform strictly to its materialism. Donald Lowrie describes the two essential beliefs of the

Marxist materialist creed: "They were, on the one hand, insistence that man's fate is determined wholly by economic materialism, and on the other, the passionate messianic faith that a time would come when, in a perfect society, man would no longer be dependent upon economics" (44). But Berdyaev found more untenable contradiction than acceptable paradox in such Marxist ideas as "the recognition of necessity," whereby man is free when he acts in the only way possible (Mathewson 145). As Berdyaev summed up his view of rationalism, "It may be that the laws of logic which hold us in such a vise are only an illness of being, a defect in being itself" (Lowrie 108). The religious philosopher Chaadaev had expressed a similar idea earlier in the century: "What is logical analysis if not an act of violence which the spirit performs upon itself?" (Lowrie 68). Like Wright and Ellison, Berdyaev preserved some of the social lessons from his Marxist association; early in his career he announced, "I finally move from positivism to metaphysical idealism, and in conformity with this I change my attitude toward Marxism, from which I still retain a series of realistic social ideas but which I deny as a whole world-view," adding later that "a mystical consciousness of personality has always been the basic motive of my life" (Lowrie 95, 96). Berdyaev's intense consciousness of his personal mission of serving human dignity, itself influenced to a large degree by Dostoevsky, is paralleled by similar explicit statements of Richard Wright and Ralph Ellison.

II

Despite the fact that Dostoevsky's early commitment to socialism included a strong Christian element, his first novels, *Poor Folk* and *The Double*, reflect a vacillation and an apparent irresolution between the notions of freedom and determinism, i.e., between individual and environmental causation. But although the now atheistic Belinsky exerted pressure on Dostoevsky to modify or abandon his concentration on individual dignity for more emphasis on social protest, it seems that especially in *The Double* Dostoevsky had found his lifelong concern in depicting the suffering which the individual can cause himself by refusing the responsibility of freedom. Some evidence suggests that the influence of Belinsky's determinism and atheism may have contributed to Dostoevsky's vacillation during a critical period in the mid-to-late 1840s. But Dostoevsky's involvement with the radical Petrashevsky group, some of whose members were militant materialists and atheists, apparently was guided by the principles of Christian socialism he had imbibed years before. The Dostoevsky who was arrested, tried, and sentenced to Siberia for his rather minimal radical activity seems already to have rejected, without ever having fully adopted, determinism and materialism. Certain statements by Dostoevsky in the retrospective light of the 1870s suggest that he had been won over in the late forties to Belinsky's materialism and atheism. But Joseph Frank observes that these somewhat misleading comments were intended by Dostoevsky more as a polemical position on the supposed incompatibility of socialism and Christianity, than as an attempt at strict autobiographical fact (191).

While some of Dostoevsky's youthful literary influences, especially those of Hugo and Balzac, fired his devotion to social reform and humanitarianism, others stamped on him an aversion to materialism and an abiding sense of the sacred calling of art which later would help him deflect the temptations of determinism and mere social protest. Dostoevsky deeply admired Hugo, whose work had become a symbol of the social humanitarianism that followed the revolution of 1830. Balzac had an even greater impact on Dostoevsky, for his works combined visionary social concern with interior dramas dealing with broad ranges of moral experience (Frank 107). Dostoevsky's adolescent love of Schiller, whose egoism he would later parody but whose idealism he would always venerate, presumably led Dostoevsky to his first encounter with and his rejection of eighteenth-century materialism, which the character Franz Moor used as a justification for his villainy (Frank 61). Schelling's view of art as an organ of metaphysical cognition profoundly affected Dostoevsky and the entire generation of the forties, most of whom believed in the metaphysical mission of art (Frank 64). Although Dostoevsky accepted the doctrine of protest-minded ''social realism'' as advocated by Belinsky in the forties, he always retained his view formed under Romantic influence of the literary creative act as sacred and inviolable (Frank 180).

Dostoevsky's socialism, assimilated several years before he met Belinsky, was essentially of the Christian variety, whose leading spokesmen had come from France in the thirties and forties. Though not completely orthodox, Dostoevsky's beliefs were identifiably Christian, as Joseph Frank suggests in discussing a comment of Dostoevsky's linking Homer and Christ:

> The youthful Dostoevsky can hardly be accused of any simple-minded acceptance of conventional religious notions; his words smack much more of the Utopian Socialist doctrine of religion as "progressive revelation" than of Christian orthodoxy. Dostoevsky's thought seems to be that Christ had proclaimed "the organization of spiritual and earthly life" for modernity, and that Homer, inspired by this divine source, was expressing in his poetry the true meaning of Christ's teaching. This would indicate that Dostoevsky's Christianity had already become strongly social and humanitarian, and was practically identical with what was being called "socialism" in France. (110)

Dowler adds that ''Socialism represented to Dostoevsky and his contemporaries an idealistic humanitarianism which they hailed as the natural successor to

Christianity" (67). Dostoevsky viewed Christ not just as a revolutionary, as was rather common in the 1840s, but as the divine augur of man's freedom from historical determinism. Influenced by his good friend Maikov, Dostoevsky understood Christ both as the traditional savior from sin and as the promise of moral freedom (Frank 210). Maikov died in 1847, but Dostoevsky evidently remained a Utopian (i.e., theological or Christian) rather than a revolutionary socialist up to the time of his arrest in 1849 (Dowler 67). At the time, then, when Dostoevsky met Belinsky in 1845, not only did he know that Christianity and socialism were historically and presently compatible; he himself had been a serious subscriber to the fusion of the two for several years.

During the few years when Dostoevsky's evidently solid Christian social-ism clashed with Belinsky's evolving atheism, Dostoevsky learned of the potential conflict between his religious faith and his socialist convictions (or perhaps those of others). Through part of their two-year friendship from 1845 to 1847, Belinsky was in a process, as discussed above, of relinquishing his moral-religious sentiments and gravitating toward rationalism and his final position of atheism. His interest in Left Hegelianism, which was primarily a critique of religion, led Belinsky to reject his previously held Utopian socialist convictions and to announce his atheism (Frank 185). Though the diametrical opposition of Dostoevsky's and Belinsky's world-views did not become immediately clear because of their common goal of socialism and their concern for unfortunates, the disagreement over belief caused great strain and, finally, the rupture of their relationship. In *The Notebooks to The Devils* Dostoevsky reminisces about the conflict: "I remember the writer D., then still almost a boy, whom Belinsky was trying to convert to atheism. When D. would raise any objections in Christ's defense, Belinsky would abuse Christ in the vilest terms" (93). In a note from his *Diary of a Writer,* he remarks of Belinsky, "I found him a passionate Socialist, and he began immediately with me on atheism" (Frank 192). Dostoevsky's great success with his first work, *Poor Folk*, had been crowned with Belinsky's critical acclaim. But Dostoevsky's membership in the latter's literary group became a bitter experience because its members mocked Dostoevsky's vanity and because Dostoevsky and Belinsky found their differences growing more profound (Frank 171). The literary implications of their conflicting metaphysical views inevitably presented themselves; as Belinsky's social realism took a step backward to a utilitarian "aesthetic," Dostoevsky's aesthetic remained deeply metaphysical and spiritual. As Dostoevsky explained later, he quarreled with Belinsky

> because of ideas about literature and of the tendency of literature. My view was radically opposed to Belinsky's view. I blamed him for trying to give literature a partial significance unworthy of it, leveling it solely to the description, if one may express it so, only of journalistic facts or scandalous occurrences. (Frank 181)

Both *Poor Folk*, published in 1845, just before Dostoevsky met Belinsky, and *The Double*, published in 1846, in the middle of their association, reflect Belinsky's influence as well as what might be construed as some degree of indecision on the issue of social determinism. But the basic thrust of *The Double* points toward the end of their relationship and toward the resolution of Dostoevsky's conflict on the side of the individual personality rather than environment. Belinsky's somewhat misled championing of Gogol in the early forties as primarily a critic of social injustices resulted in Belinsky's prescription of social realism for the evolving Russian literature. *Poor Folk*, written in the shadow of Gogol and of Belinsky's influential criticism, implies that the misery of the "little men" like Makar Devushkin is caused by an oppressive social environment. But in a larger sense the novel contains the same spiritual plea as found in the French social novel of the thirties and in Dickens, that those with power recognize their moral duty toward their less fortunate brothers (Frank 147). Frank comments on the issue of human dignity raised in the scene where a button falls off Devushkin's coat and rolls on the floor and his superior shakes Devushkin's hand:

> The stress laid on this motif shows Dostoevsky's acute awareness

that the spiritual is of equal importance with the material in alleviating the lot of the unfortunates--even, perhaps, of greater importance, since poverty only heightens the need for self-esteem and self-respect to the point of morbidity. . . . In *Poor Folk*, this tension between the spiritual and the material is still latent and in a state of equilibrium; the emphasis accorded the spiritual (or, if one prefers, the moral-psychological) dimension of human experience only heightens the pathos of the material injustices that Dostoevsky's characters have to suffer. (147)

The Double presents a fascinating depiction of one individual's loss of all sense of dignity and sanity. Seemingly because its psychological observations combine with subtle social protest, the novel met with faint praise and stinging criticism from Belinsky. Yet at this point Dostoevsky clearly had not abandoned completely Belinsky's determinist-tinged doctrine of realism. Frank points out the ambiguity of tone in Dostoevsky's work of this period, where a character is shown as both socially oppressed and as morally unsavory because of his surrender to the forces of his environment:

More and more Dostoevsky became concerned with the psychic distortions suffered in the struggle of the personality to assert itself and to satisfy the natural human need for dignity and self-respect in a world of rigid class barriers and political despotism. But so long as his stories continued to use the familiar iconography of the Natural School, a social causation was always at least implied for the psychic malformation of his characters--even if not stressed sufficiently to satisfy Belinsky. (366)

An interesting point of conjecture regarding Dostoevsky's vacillation over such fundamental issues during these years is whether a mysterious nervous illness which afflicted him was caused by the apparent suspension of his final choice between freedom and determinism, faith and unbelief, individuality and solidarity. As he recalled later,

Two years before Siberia, at the time of various literary difficulties and quarrels, I was the victim of some sort of strange and unbearably torturing nervous illness. I cannot tell you what these

> hideous sensations were, but I remember them vividly; it often
> seemed to me that I was dying, and the truth is--real death came
> and then went away again. (Frank 167)

Though possibly a harbinger of the epilepsy which began to afflict Dostoevsky in Siberia, these particular symptoms did not recur after he resolved this ambivalence. Frank analyzes what he sees as the healthy tension between Dostoevsky's "two Romanticisms," Christianity and French socialism: "The former concentrates on the inner struggle of the soul for purification; the latter combats the degrading influence of a brutalizing environment" (111).

Dostoevsky's radical activity in the late 1840s, though relatively brief and rather mild, still constituted a serious commitment to action rather than just utopian discussion; but it seems that he never defected from his Christian principles to materialistic and revolutionary activism. He associated first with the Beketov circle, a Utopian socialist group headed by one of his few good friends from engineering school. This affiliation, together with Dostoevsky's friendship with Maikov, reinforced his religious outlook:

> Far from being a political innocent, abruptly baptized into social-
> ism, atheism, and materialism all at once by the great intellectual
> agitator Belinsky, Dostoevsky was a committed moral-religious
> progressive who stoutly maintained his convictions in the face of
> Belinsky's attacks and then allied himself with others of the same
> persuasion. (Frank 201)

Dostoevsky also came to frequent the meetings of the largely but not exclusively atheistic Petrashevsky circle, as much out of the need for companionship and lively conversation as for anything else, especially as his stock had fallen quite low with Belinsky and his literary group. Petrashevsky himself, who openly scoffed at Christ with references such as "the well-known demagogue, whose career finished rather unsuccessfully" (Frank 242), produced on Dostoevsky, according to a member of the group "a repulsive impression because he was an atheist and mocked at faith" (Frank 247). In the wake of the failed revolutions of 1848, the Petrashevsky circle became increasingly radical, and some of its members plotted to set up and operate a secret printing press. Dostoevsky became one of this sub-group and accepted the responsibility of actively recruiting on its behalf. He had been tutored in radical activism by the organizer of this sub-group, a magnetic personality and atheist named Speshnev. Dostoevsky's deeper radical involvement was preceded and, perhaps, caused by what he interpreted as a strange sort of moral entrapment: "I have taken money from Speshnev (about 500 roubles), and now I am *with him* and *his*. I'll never be able to pay back such a sum, yes, and he wouldn't take the money back; that's the kind of man he is. . . . Do you understand, from now on I have a Mephistopheles of my own" (Frank 270). In his *Diary of a Writer*, written in the 1870s, Dostoevsky indicated that he never could have become a "Nechaev," the leader of a secret group that had murdered one of its members in 1869, "but as for my becoming a Nechaevets, I can't certify, perhaps, possibly, . . . in the days of my youth" (Frank 269). Thus Dostoevsky took considerable risk in the attempt to concretize his Christian-socialist principles, and he paid the price of four years' penal servitude and four years' exile in Siberia. The offense had not been merely his reading Belinsky's "Letter to Gogol" (a highly ironic situation) at a meeting, as is often reported, but actually had entailed a substantial degree of radical commitment if not of overt action.

Even at the height of his activism in league with atheists such as Speshnev, Dostoevsky retained his fundamentally Christian outlook and deprecated deterministic socialism. At one of the secret meetings in April 1949, shortly before his arrest, he is quoted as having placed his emphasis on the freedom and the moral duty of the individual: "One should not condemn society, and should work on it not by gall and mockery but by revealing one's own shortcomings." A draft version of these words reads: "that before condemning one should be better oneself" (Frank 282). His last works before his arrest, the short story "The Landlady" and the unfinished novel *Netochka Nezvanova*, duplicate this shift of responsibility from society to the moral failings of individuals (Frank 283). One of Dostoevsky's statements at his trial reflects his clear disapproval of materialistic socialism, which by 1849 had virtually eliminated moral-religious socialism as a movement:

> Precisely because I do not adhere to any of the social systems, I studied Socialism in general, all of its systems, and this is why I see the faults in every social system. I am convinced that the application of any of them would bring with it inescapable ruin, and I am not talking about us but even in France. (Frank 252)

In his deposition after arrest he spoke negatively of the "relentless necessity of Fourierism," a branch of determinist socialism (Frank 254). His asking brother Mikhail for a Bible while waiting to be sent to Siberia further suggests his frame of mind at the conclusion of his association with proponents of determinism and materialism (Maurina 51).

Dostoevsky made several later references to his radicalism, some of which tend to misrepresent his relationship with Belinsky as a seduction into deterministic and atheistic thought. In an 1870s account of his youthful tendency to understand human vices too narrowly in social and political terms, Dostoevsky seems to estimate fairly the blinkering effects of his radicalism. He comments on the beating of a peasant without reason by a government courier: "Never was I able to forget the courier, and much that was shameful and cruel in the Russian people I was then inclined for a long while, as it were involuntarily, to explain in an obviously much too one-sided fashion" (Frank 72). While writing *The Devils* in 1870, Dostoevsky confided in a letter that even during his prison term he held some traces of his "liberalism":

> Last winter I happened to read a serious admission in a leading article in the *Golos*--that we "almost rejoiced during the Crimean War at the success of the Allied arms and at the defeat of our own." No, my Radicalism did not go so far as that; at that time I was still serving my time in the galleys and did *not* rejoice at the success of the Allies; but together with my comrades, the unhappy ones and their soldier-guards, I felt myself a Russian, I wished success to Russian arms--although I still retained a strong leaven of scabby Russian liberalism, preached by ones like the dung-beetle Belinsky

and the rest, I did not consider myself inconsistent, when I felt the Russian in myself. (*Letters* 91)

But a misleading depiction of Dostoevsky's experience in the 1840s evidently was conveyed in some articles in *Diary of a Writer* in 1873, where he implied that Belinsky had converted him to atheism and materialism and that socialism and Christianity had always been fundamentally incompatible. As demonstrated above, though, Dostoevsky had held his theological ground against Belinsky's proselytizing; and Dostoevsky's commitment to Christian socialism years before he met Belinsky belies his later implication that socialism in Russia had been from its inception atheistic and anti-Christian (Frank 191). The fusion of socialism and atheism in Russia had occurred with Belinsky's conversion to the latter, and this fusion had only grown more pronounced through the nihilistic sixties and early seventies. Dostoevsky therefore "had come to see Belinsky as the symbolic source of the Russian nihilism that the novelist had battled with all through the 1860s, and against which he had just launched his most violently anti-radical work, *The Devils*" (Frank 183). Belinsky had in fact introduced Dostoevsky to atheistic socialism, and

> this was the only kind that the Dostoevsky of the 1870s believed to be spiritually honest and intellectually self-consistent. . . . The tendencies evident in the later Belinsky had hardened into dogma, and it was impossible any longer to be a radical and to continue to affirm the existence of free will. In the 1870s, when there was a return of the moral-religious Feuerbachian "humanism" of the 1840s among the Russian left, Dostoevsky's hostility became considerably mollified. (Frank 211)

Vaclav Cerny's legitimate objection to Dostoevsky's tying socialism and atheism together parallels that of Frank; but in light of the facts on Dostoevsky's first-hand knowledge of Christian socialism, Cerny's question seems rather naive: "When we see Dostoevsky curse socialism for its atheism, we ask if he knew that in the West atheistic socialism existed alongside the socialism of faith, that against Fourier and Saint-Simon stood the socialism of George Sand, Bulloz, and Lammenais" (45). Although the Dostoevsky who was taken in a convict sled to Siberia in 1849 would never again give consideration to a viewpoint that incorporated radicalism or materialism, he would remain faithful to Christian socialism's spirit of universal fraternity throughout his life.

III

After Dostoevsky's removal from the literary scene for ten years, from 1849 to 1859, he began the first stage of his career-long attack on the intertwined ideologies of materialistic and Utilitarian socialism and atheism with *The House of the Dead* (1862), a psychological record of his prison experiences; *Winter Notes on Summer Impressions* (1862), a short personal critique of Western socialism; and *Notes from Underground* (1864), a much fuller indictment of the arrogance and inadequacy of Utilitarian socialism and all rationalist system-building. Though in this first stage he would focus mainly on materialist socialism, later Dostoevsky would concentrate on its ideological descendants, nihilism (in *Crime and Punishment*) as well as anarchism, moral relativism, and atheism (in *The Devils* and *The Brothers Karamazov*). Cerny suggests the underlying unity of these various ideological demons which Dostoevsky sought to exorcise from Russia:

> He went after the common denominator, the basic universal sin whose refutation would put all to shame. He locates, whether rightly or wrongly, this common denominator in hard-core materialism and, consequently, in atheism, the denial of God and his law, which indeed logically follows from materialism. (47)

In terms of this discussion thus far, the first three post-Siberian works figure as a decisive break with Dostoevsky's earlier vacillation over, and concessions to the deterministic attitude implicit in Belinsky's social realism.

The House of the Dead (or, more literally, *Notes from a Dead House*), despite its being cast in fictional form as the memoirs of a man who had served ten years for murdering his wife, serves quite transparently as Dostoevsky's meditation on his experiences in prison and on the nature of the Russian people and of man in general. Although one of its themes is the brutalizing effect of the "compulsory communism" (Jackson, *Art* 50) of prison life, Dostoevsky wrote *not* a protest work but a conscious examination of the psychological and spiritual effects of such life on men, and he observes the diverse expressions of personality and dignity in an environment seemingly devoid of freedom. Robert Jackson refers to *The House of the Dead* as "the great divide in Dostoevsky's works" (*Dostoevsky* 159), for its conclusions on freedom, environment, and individual dignity serve as the basis for all his later writing. But Jackson overestimates the idea of environment as Dostoevsky presents it:

> The dead house for him became a metaphor for an enclosed, godless universe. . . . The concept of a dead house contains the notion of a universe that is indeed dominated by fate and in which man is a helpless prey to the forces of accident. Yet the convict's entire behavior represents an unconscious protest against the idea of a meaningless universe. It is a protest, however, in which he is not ennobled, but humiliated. (*Dostoevsky* 15, 160)

Dostoevsky's central thesis in *The House of the Dead* holds that no matter how oppressive or controlled the environment or conditions of existence, man sooner or later will assert his dignity, will act in a manner perhaps even contrary to his self-interest so long as he has an opportunity to express his humanity and individuality. Dostoevsky's convict protests not against the "meaninglessness" of his small and rigid universe (for he often recognizes the appropriateness of it, or is simply resigned to his placement there), but against its tendency to deny and quash all traces of his individuality. Perhaps this work's seminal idea for the development of Dostoevsky's subsequent fiction comes from his observation that perverse and self-harming acts are sometimes desperate but nonetheless spiritual expressions of personality and paradoxically of human dignity; that they are therefore in a sense ''necessary'' assertions of freedom, choices of the individual to battle the outrages of one dehumanizing environment or another. They are choices which, even if they issue in defeat or the disfiguration of a whole personality, still somehow ennoble the human being because of his refusal to become a machine.

Both Wright and Ellison later would respond to *The House of the Dead* as a metaphor for any oppressive and threatening environment, which invites, and in a sense demands, all manner of perverse acts of rebellion and self-destruction as expressions of a free personality. Two examples are Bigger Thomas's killing of Bessie Mears, his black girlfriend, in *Native Son* and Tod Clifton's suicidal confrontation with the policeman in *Invisible Man*. But although Dostoevsky clearly argues that the power of environment *is* transcended, and can even be overcome by the free human personality, both Wright and Ellison clung for a time to the conviction of environment's superiority.

Dostoevsky thus establishes the squarely anti-determinist stance of *The House of the Dead* when his memoirist Goryanchikov locates the intense need for, and the existence of freedom at the heart of brutal prison life. One finds here the germ of an idea which will reach full development thirty years later in ''The Grand Inquisitor,'' that is, the potentially crushing weight of freedom on the individual:

> Some who came to the prison were men who had lost their heads, had become too reckless when at liberty, so that at last they committed their crimes as it were irresponsibly, as it were without an object, as it were in a delirium, in intoxication. . . . ''We are a lost lot,'' they used to say; ''since we didn't know how to get on in freedom now we must walk the Green Street.'' (38)

But the infrequency of the feeling of freedom in prison, and the strangeness of its manifestations, becomes Dostoevsky's focus: ''Nothing can be more curious than these strange outbreaks of impatience and revolt. Often a man is patient for several years, is resigned, endures most cruel punishment, and suddenly breaks out over some little thing, some trifle, a mere nothing'' (41). Dostoevsky relates the story of a prisoner, distinguished for his mild behavior, who one day without warning or reason attacked a sergeant and afterward as he lay dying ''said that he never meant any harm to anyone, but was only seeking suffering'' (60). Through his protagonist-speaker Dostoevsky concludes the primacy of the personality's spiritual need for expression:

> Possibly the cause of this sudden outbreak, in the man from whom one would least have expected it, is simply the poignant hysterical craving for self-expression, the unconscious yearning for himself, the desire to assert himself, to assert his crushed personality, a desire which suddenly takes possession of him and reaches the pitch of fury, of spite, of mental aberration, of fits and nervous convulsions. (113)

The hope for the transcendence of such conditions lies in individuals' innate demand for respect as human beings, as best illustrated in the healing moral effect on the convicts in their enjoyment of their own theatrical productions.

Admitting the horrible depths of degradation to which a person can sink in any environment, Dostoevsky stoutly posits the individual's ultimate responsibility for his spiritual condition. He notes of the convict Orlov, "what horrified me was the spiritual deadness of the man. . . . At the first glance you could see from his face that nothing was left but a fierce lust of physical gratification--sensuality, gluttony" (86). His summary of another, whom he designates as A., "a moral Quasimodo," emphasizes the element of personal accountability: "He was the most revolting example of the depths to which a man can sink and degenerate, and the extent to which he can destroy all moral feeling in himself without difficulty or repentance" (107). As Dostoevsky would write in his notebook in 1863: "Man changes not for external reasons but for no other reason than from moral change" (Dowler 134). The most concise statement of Dostoevsky's theme occurs in Goryanchikov's summary:

> It is high time we gave up apathetic complaints of being corrupted by the environment. It is true that it does destroy a great deal in

us, but not everything, and often a crafty and knowing rogue, especially if he is an eloquent speaker or writer, will cover up not simply weakness but often real baseness, justifying it by the influence of his "environment." (224)

Though early in *The House of the Dead* Dostoevsky observes a general lack of guilt or repentance, and doubts "whether one of the convicts even admitted his lawlessness" (38), in later years he sought to counter the implication that the convicts felt caught up in a destiny beyond their control. In a section of *Diary of a Writer* called "Environment," Dostoevsky made even more explicit his rejection of determinism and of fatalism as an attribute of the Russian people:

> The people call the criminals "unfortunates" and extend charity to them. Is there expressed here the Christian truth or the truth of "environment"? Now right here one may find the stumbling block, the concealed lever which the propagandist of "environment" might seize upon with success. No, the people do not deny crime and they know that the criminal is guilty. They simply mean to say: "You have sinned and are suffering, but we too are sinners. If we were in your place, perhaps we might have done worse. If we ourselves were better, perhaps you would not have been sitting in prison. Pray for us and we will pray for you." (Jackson, *Dostoevsky* 141)

In one of his most significant statements on environment, Dostoevsky points to Christianity as assisting the individual immeasurably by making resistance to environment his moral duty:

> Christianity, while fully recognizing the pressure of environment and declaring forgiveness to the sinner, nonetheless makes man's struggle with environment a moral duty, draws a line where environment ends and duty begins. Making people responsible, Christianity at the same time recognizes their freedom. (Jackson, *Dostoevsky* 142)

Winter Notes on Summer Impressions, an essay written on Dostoevsky's two-month tour of Europe and England in 1862, argues that Western socialism cannot succeed because of its denial of true individuality and its diminishment of individual freedom for "'progress''' and comfort. Dostoevsky acknowledges the West's impressive material accomplishment, but claims that it is purchased at the price of "'a systematic, submissive, fostered loss of consciousness''' (93). He criticizes Western socialism for its assumption that fraternity can be created by a mechanistic and self-centered ideology such as Utilitarianism:

> The Westerner speaks of fraternity as of a great motivating force of humankind, and does not understand that it is impossible to obtain fraternity if it does not exist in reality. What is to be done? Fraternity must be obtained at any cost. But as it happens it is impossible to create fraternity, for it creates itself, comes of itself, exists in nature. But in French nature, and in Occidental nature in general, it is not present; you find there instead a principle of individualism, a principle of isolation, of intense self-isolation, of intense self-preservation, of personal gain, of self-determination of the I, of opposing this I to all nature and the rest of mankind. (111)

As Dowler points out, the attempt of Western socialist society to generate some semblance of brotherhood would invite "'the eventual eradication of individual liberty in the socialist anthill'' (80). Prefiguring the rebellion of *Notes from Underground*, Dostoevsky adds that for such a utopia man will refuse to surrender "'a tiny drop of his freedom for the common welfare. . . . He keeps on thinking that this is a prison, that it is better to be independent, because there is complete free will'' (114).

Notes from Underground, Dostoevsky's work which contributed much in terms of basic situation, tone, and theme to Wright's "The Man Who Lived Underground" and Ellison's *Invisible Man*, mounts an idealist and existentialist critique of rationalism and materialism and serves as the prologue to his major novels, especially *Crime and Punishment, The Devils,* and *The Brothers Karamazov.* Dostoevsky finds absolutely untenable rationalism's violation of the individual; he argues that the irrational or supra-rational component of man's being will never submit to the materialist definition of man or to any attempt to construct a certifiably rational, collectivized society. *Notes from*

Underground signals the end of his effort toward reconciliation between radical Westernizers and conservative Slavophiles. Dostoevsky and Grigoryev, with their modestly successful native soil movement, sought to take advantage of the unusual fluidity in Russian society in the early 1860s to effect, according to Dostoevsky, a union of "civilization with the national principle" (Dowler 91). The journal *Vremya,* edited by Dostoevsky and his brother Mikhail, demonstrated the open-mindedness of the "men of the soil" by embracing several progressive causes and by criticizing Slavophile narrowness (Dowler 96). But as the stridency of the radicals began to develop into nihilism, and as Dostoevsky came to interpret the radicals' now exclusive adherence to materialism as a threat to the individual, he renounced what might be called his post-Siberian period of fairness to the new crop of radicals. Whether *Notes from Underground* represents a recanting of beliefs Dostoevsky had held earlier is doubtful, but it seems clear that the work involves his final act of "writing off" the radicals as a possible part of his personal program for the advancement of Russia. He had refrained from direct or harsh criticism of leading radicals such as Chernyshevsky, but with *Notes from Underground* he unleashes his anti-hero as a polemical retort to the saintly but lifeless ideal of heroism in Chernyshevsky's novel *What Is to Be Done?*

Dostoevsky's perverse, morbid, impotent, and self-pitying protagonist in *Notes from Underground* discusses and embodies what he aptly calls "the pleasure of despair" (95), which Kierkegaard analyzes in *The Sickness Unto Death* with a similar affirmation of the supreme worth of the individual. The underground man consciously revolts against the materialist's regarding all human subjectivity, including notions of virtue and dignity, as "ravings and superstitions" (98). Though Dostoevsky distances himself from the underground man's egoism and self-destructive individualism, he favors the development of this sort of personality over that of an automaton. Through his "hero," writing from his "mousehole," Dostoevsky ridicules Utilitarian utopianism's smug pigeonholing of human possibility and its arrogant ignorance of man's refusal to sacrifice self-expression and individual freedom for any rigid system, no matter how benevolently intended. Though the protagonist is not a Christian himself, his belief in impossibility serves as a metaphor for all human subjectivity and hints at the conversion to Christ which Dostoevsky had included in the work's pre-censored version: "Of course, I won't be able to breach this wall with my head if I'm not strong enough. But I don't have to accept a stone wall just because it's there and I don't have the strength to breach it" (99). Over against the Utilitarians' preachment that all men will act rationally and predictably once such behavior is shown to be in their self-interest, the underground man sets the observation that a human's "last advantage" is his unique and ultimate freedom to act for *or against* his comfort and well-being:

> So one's own free, unrestrained choice, one's own whim, be it the wildest, one's own fancy, sometimes worked up to a frenzy--that is the most advantageous advantage that cannot be fitted into any table or scale and that causes every system and every theory to crumble into dust on contact. . . . All man actually needs is independent will, at all costs and whatever the consequences. (110)

As will be discussed below, although Wright's and Ellison's underground men, Fred Daniels and the Invisible Man, do not share this man's deep psychic displacement, all three begin in flight from a merciless environment, undergo a kind of death, and learn of their boundless freedom and its accompanying weight of responsibility.

Chapter 2

Wright's and Ellison's Radical Commitment
and Drifting from Naturalism

Although neither Wright nor Ellison, unlike Dostoevsky, became involved in revolutionary radicalism or risked a death sentence or a prison term for his activity, each made a commitment for a time to the radical Communist Party, whose materialist and determinist creed parallels that of the radical socialists that Dostoevsky began to refute with *The House of the Dead, Winter Notes on Summer Impressions,* and *Notes from Underground.* Wright and Ellison, responding to the Party's vaunted ideals and promises of social justice for all, and to its attention to their fledgling literary efforts, attempted to reconcile their first dim perceptions that a materialistic ideology tends to minimize the concrete realization of individual freedom and dignity. Even their early fiction, written during each man's closest connection to the Party, betrays doubt about the benevolence of any white organization, especially an authoritarian one, and shows more faith in black nationalist feeling than in rigid rationalist applications of economic theory. This chapter first will trace Wright's and Ellison's knowledge of and conscious debt to Dostoevsky. Then it will provide a sketch of the background of American communism and socialism, as well as of literary naturalism, in which the writers matured. Finally, it will discuss both writers' specific affiliations with communism, their early fiction reflecting this influence, and the first stages of their disaffection with the movement.

I

When Ellison met Wright in New York in 1936, he became friends with the older and more established writer, whose work would exert a great influence on his own and with whom he would share perhaps their strongest literary link, Dostoevsky. Although Wright was several years older than Ellison and had more assurance as an artist, the men were in quite a similar situation: they were, as Robert O'Meally notes, "radically inclined black intellectuals with southern backgrounds trying to survive in New York and struggling to make art in the midst of the Great Depression" (30). Ellison's career began when his review of a novel was accepted by a magazine which Wright edited. Wright cautioned his friend against hoping for too much and gave his candid opinion that Ellison had begun his development as a writer too.late (*Shadow* 30). Soon after their meeting, in a combination of circumstances which would symbolize a central conflict in the works of both men, Wright introduced Ellison to the letters of Dostoevsky and to the local Communist Party, accompanying his younger colleague to a fund-raising affair for the Spanish Loyalists (Bone 22).

Both Wright and Ellison had a knowledge of Dostoevsky that was early and extensive, and both owed him a conscious debt that would be evident in much of their fiction. Herbert Hill cites a specific instance of influence and a more general affinity between the Russian and the two black Americans:

> Clearly Dostoevsky's *Notes from Underground* engaged the imagination of both Ellison and Wright. Both these writers were drawn to the morbidly fascinating world of Dostoevsky, not simply because their own characters are the helpless prey of a vast, senseless social order which destroys its victims, but, more importantly, because of their great concern with meaning, with identity, and with the necessity to remain sane in a society where the individual personality is denied and the world appears devoid of meaning. The work of Wright and Ellison suggests that perhaps the art of the grotesque, of fantasy, corresponds closely to the

experience of the Negro in the United States, and perhaps that is why some Negro writers have been drawn to the imagery of Dostoevsky and sense the value of the absurd and the grotesque in the works of Kafka and Joyce. (8)

By 1927 Wright had read *Poor Folk*, Dostoevsky's first novel, partly a moving story of personal loss and partly an indictment of a rigid social environment (Fabre, *Quest* 68). Margaret Walker Alexander, a friend of Wright's in the thirties, offers her recollection of Dostoevsky's early and considerable influence on him:

> It is very important to remember that way back there in the thirties, Wright was very interested in Nietzsche, Schopenhauer, and above all, the novelist Dostoevsky. Wright and I differed keenly on our taste and interest in the Russian writers. He believed that Dostoevsky was the greatest novelist who ever lived and that *The Brothers Karamazov* was his greatest novel. (Ray, 53)

In *American Hunger* Wright confides that reading *The Devils* "revealed new realms of feeling" for him (19). While Wright lived with friends Herbert and Jane Newton and worked at completing *Native Son,* he was encouraged by Jane to reread with close attention to technique and detail both *The Devils* and *The Brothers Karamazov* (Fabre, *Quest* 175). Alexander offers a suggestion that Wright's influence on modern writers parallels that of Gogol on Russian writers of the nineteenth century: "Like the Russians, who say they have all come out of Gogol's 'Overcoat,' most of our writers have come out of Wright's cloak" (Ray, 66).

Ellison has been a lifelong student of Dostoevsky and also of nineteenth-century Russian literature in general. In an interview Ellison once explained that he derived his way of looking at his material not through sociology but "through literature: English, French, Spanish, Russian--especially nineteenth-century Russian literature" (List 57). In 1937, a year after meeting Wright, Ellison hunted and sold game in Dayton, Ohio, to earn a living; at night he wrote and studied Dostoevsky, among others (*Shadow* 169), who taught him the use

44

of dreams in fiction (O'Meally 30). In describing his growing disaffection with the Communist Party, he notes that "they hated Dostoevsky, but I was always studying Dostoevsky. I was also reading Marx, Gorky, Sholokhov, and Isaac Babel" (Neal 64). Ellison frequently makes connections in his essays between Russian literature and black experience, for example his observation that Wright's *Black Boy* recalls *The House of the Dead* (*Shadow* 201). He also states that "the extent of beatings and psychological maimings meted out by Southern Negro parents rivals those described by the nineteenth-century Russian writers as characteristic of peasant life under the Czars" (*Shadow* 210). Ellison's understanding of the crucial importance of folklore to the development of Russian literature carries over in his growing promulgation of black folklore through the late 1930s and 1940s (*Shadow* 171). His service as an Instructor in Russian Literature at Bard College from 1958 to 1961 further suggests his interest and expertise in the area (Reilly 115). In an interview with John Hersey, Ellison spoke at length and quite specifically about the similarity of social disruption and consequent fluidity in nineteenth-century Russia and mid-twentieth-century America:

> Some writers--say Dostoevsky, or even Tolstoy--will make you very much aware of what is possible in depicting a society in which class lines are either fluid or have broken down without the cultural style and values of either extreme being dissipated. From such writers you learn to explore the rich fictional possibilities to be achieved in juxtaposing the peasant's consciousness with that of the aristocrat. This insight is useful when you are dealing with American society. . . .
> I would think that the access to the primary feelings that the great Russian novelists had grew out of the nature of their society and the extreme disruption of hierarchical relationships which occurred during the nineteenth century. . . . Such disruptions of the traditional ordering of society, as in our own country since 1954, made for an atmosphere of irrationality, and this created an unrestrained expressiveness. Eyeballs were peeled, nerves were laid bare, and private sensibilities were subjected to public laceration. In fact, life became so theatrical (not to say nightmarish) that

even Dostoevsky's smoking imagination was barely able to keep a step ahead of what was actually happening in the garrets and streets. Today, here in the United States, we have something similar, but there's no point in my trying to explain Russian extremism, or the genius of the great nineteenth-century Russian novelists. Not even Dostoevsky was able to do that. ("Personality" 16)

Thus Ellison and Wright had a conscious debt to Dostoevsky both in terms of craft and social analysis.

II

Wright and Ellison took part in the general leftward turn of American intellectuals and artists of the 1920s and 1930s, a time of unusually open criticism of American political, economic, and social organization. The socialist tradition in American life can be traced to early- and mid-nineteenth-century utopian communities, from which blacks were excluded (Foner 6). When socialists came to address the issue of black Americans late in the century, they argued that blacks were just workers like white workers and therefore suffered no special oppression aside from that of all workers under capitalism (Foner 72). In the 1890s some socialists both black and white, influenced by Russian anarchists of the eighties, advocated an anarchistic doctrine of "propaganda by deed" (Foner 81). The nineties also saw the contrasting development of Christian socialism, which called for a system of social and political relations based on love of God and man. However, the Christian socialist and Fabian movements gained few adherents, and by the late nineties were all but defunct. Yet the gradual, peaceable approach inherent in Christian socialism had a deeper influence on black Americans than did the more radical urgings of other socialistic groups (Foner 84). Blacks' perception that mainstream American socialism was indifferent to them led to dissatisfaction evident in the founding of the NAACP in 1911. W. E. B. DuBois was a Socialist Party member for less than a year due to disillusionment with the organization's stand on the race question (Foner 218). Hubert H. Harrison, known as "the father of socialism in Harlem," broke with the Party during World War I to promote the doctrine of "race first," combining socialism and black nationalism (Foner 266).

Some liberals and radicals tended to distrust any imported systems of ideological organization. But many blacks had confidence in the fruits of the socialist revolution in Russia, feeling that the socialist perspective would eventually improve the lot of blacks generally (Foner, Allen xi). After the Bolshevik triumph in Russia, black socialists praised the revolution and noted the contrast between the elimination of Jewish pogroms in Soviet Russia and the heightening violence against blacks in the United States (Foner 275). Black socialists were impressed by Lenin's 1913 article titled "Russians and Negroes," in which he drew parallels between the feudalistic oppression of southern blacks after the Civil War and the situation of freed Russian serfs before the revolution (Foner, Allen xiii). Many American writers found Russia in the thirties to be achieving enviable progress in productivity and social reform. After the breakdown of the American economy, the Left attracted followers more easily. To "go Left" in the thirties, when Wright and Ellison became attracted to radicalism, was much more acceptable than in the twenties, when the government had arrested, jailed, or deported many "alien radicals" (Foner 312).

The mood of black radicalism intensified after World War I, as disgusted black soldiers returned home to experience less freedom than previously and considerably more violence in the form of beatings, lynchings, and riots. The journals *Challenge, Crusader, The Emancipator,* and *The Messenger* defined and extended this militancy. After the split in the Socialist Party and the formation of the Communist Party in 1919, the African Blood Brotherhood provided the latter with some members, largely due to the communists' more sensitive handling of the "Negro question." Still, in 1928, the Communist Party had no more than fifty black, dues-paying members worldwide. Yet it was the only white political organization in the United States where the need for black equality was raised at all (Foner, Allen xi). The "Resolution on the Negro Question" from the sixth World Congress of the Communist International implicitly recognized that racism within the Party had to be fought while it advocated full social and political equality for all black Americans (Foner, Allen xiv).

Many of the writers who joined or supported the Communist Party left it for the reason that motivated Wright and Ellison, namely its lack of respect for the individual's (and especially the artist's) autonomy and freedom. Although it promoted young writers, the Party never completely trusted them, partly due to its strong anti-intellectual bias. The most famous writers such as Dreiser, Sinclair, Steinbeck, Hemingway, MacLeish, and Wolfe were the most suspect in the Party's eyes (Aaron 309). Among other objections, Wright disagreed with the narrow, proletarian view that writers should perform menial tasks. Claude McKay, a supporter of the Russian revolution, became alienated from the American Communist Party because of its racism. Some writers left quietly, some noisily. Some made a final break when they reached a "last straw" situation; some refused to yield and waited to be thrown out (Aaron 312). Many, like Wright, severed their ties not so much with anger as with sorrow and regret.

W. E. B. DuBois and Marcus Garvey were two very influential black leaders who contributed in contrasting ways to the growth of black radicalism and nationalism. DuBois evolved from a liberal sociologist who endorsed Booker T. Washington's accommodationist position, to a radical who insisted on immediate action and social change. In *The Souls of Black Folk* (1903) he broke with Washington, claiming that the latter's system "practically accepts the alleged inferiority of the Negro" (Rudwick 69). As editor of the NAACP's *The*

Crisis, DuBois demonstrated his talent in sharp, clear, urgent articles that sought reform through activism. Yet DuBois' remoteness and intellectual austerity did not endear him to the common black folk, and he never became the savior he had imagined he would be (Rudwick 306). His influence reached its zenith in the early twenties, and the attitudes he fostered helped to prepare for the "New Negro" movement of that decade.

Marcus Garvey gained tremendous influence in the postwar years as a mass leader who was regarded as a prophet and who instilled new pride and nationalist identity into the lives of many black Americans (Foner 332). His Universal Negro Improvement Association, founded in 1919, claimed two million members, mostly migrants from the South who had become embittered by the failure of the northern promise. Like DuBois, whom he despised as seeming more white than black, Garvey became disaffected with the Socialist Party but retained a belief in socialism. Socialist leaders ultimately rejected his plan of building an African empire as unrealistic, claiming that he only drew black and white workers apart, and that he hindered black radicalism when it was gaining blacks' support (Foner 329). Garvey lacked DuBois' intellectual ability to manage his large organization, and his mishandling of his Black Star Line and other affairs led to his conviction on mail fraud and his deportation in 1927. In spite of his radical ideas and his promulgation of black pride, to some Garvey seemed to play into the hands of white racists with his insistence that the U.S. should be a white man's country and his endorsement of the Ku Klux Klan as "better friends to my race than integrationists" (Foner 332). In spite of the shortcomings of both men, their insistence and their radicalism helped to prepare for the emergence of the radicalized Wright and Ellison.

III

Throughout Wright's career one finds statements, much in the spirit of Dostoevsky, attesting to his concern with the defense of human personality. In his autobiography *American Hunger* he presents his impression of racism in terms of personality, upon first arriving in Chicago from the South: "I wondered if there had ever existed in all human history a more corroding and devastating attack upon the personalities of men than the idea of racial discrimination" (*Hunger* 5). An essay of his written in 1942 echoes this idea: "If I were asked what is the one, over-all symbol or image gained from my living that most nearly represents what I feel to be the essence of American life, I would say that it was of a man struggling mightily to free his personality from the daily and hourly encroachments of American life" (Fabre, *Quest* 243). Late in his life Wright expressed his respect for "the sacredness that I feel resides in the human personality" (Ray 137). Although Wright's tone of qualified approval of the violence in *Native Son* and *The Outsider* could be said to diminish the sense of sacredness of personality, his sincere dedication to that value led him to enlist in and then eventually defect from the Communist Party. The Party reinforced for Wright what he probably knew already as a black man in America--that capitalism frames society and smothers the individual personality. In time the Party would unwittingly teach him that communism also denies the same value.

Although Wright joined the Communist Party motivated by sincere belief in collective action, his personal and literary situation played a large part in his decision. Marxism's revolutionary call to oppressed peoples everywhere would seem to hold a natural attraction for black Americans; generally, however, they have chosen to work within the constitutional system in order to avoid Soviet influence and the inconsistent Party position on American racial issues (Brignano 51). Since the time Wright joined the Party, when only about a thousand of its 16,000 members were blacks, it has never exercised much influence over more than a small percentage of their members (Ray 40). During Wright's early days in Chicago he showed no signs of sympathy with the Party; he found himself an outsider, separated from whites by race and from blacks by his hopes for literary achievement. As he comments in *American Hunger*, "I still had no friends, casual or intimate, and felt the need for none. I had developed a self-sufficiency that kept me distant from others, emotionally and psychologically" (20). "In the capacity of an amused spectator" (61) he first attended a meeting of the radical John Reed Club in 1932, one of whose aims was to create and publish proletarian literature promoting the Communist Party. His attendance at the club meetings was motivated partly by a simple need for company, somewhat reminiscent of Dostoevsky's frequenting the Petrashevsky group: "The club was my first contact with the modern world. I had lived so utterly isolated a life that the club filled for me a need that could not be imagined by the white members who were becoming disgusted with it" (69). At first he reacted with suspicion to the communist claim of brotherhood, feeling that "Communists could not have a sincere interest in Negroes. I was cynical and I would rather have heard a white man say that he hated Negroes, which I could have readily believed, than to have heard him say that he respected Negroes" (60). As he spent more time with the club, Wright became impressed with its members' lack of condescension and found the communist analysis of the world basically sound if oversimplified. Eventually he was won over not by the economics of communism but by "the similarity of the experiences of workers in other lands, by the possibility of uniting scattered but kindred peoples into a whole" (63). He describes a pivotal experience of watching crowds at a relief station, where he first recognized that possibility:

> Their talking was enabling them to sense the collectivity of their lives, and some of their fear was passing. . . . Yes, some of the things that the Communists said were true; they maintained that there came times in history when a ruling class could no longer rule, and I sat looking at the beginnings of anarchy. (44)

Within two months of joining the John Reed Club, Wright was elected secretary, an action he later interpreted as manipulative on the part of the Club: "Though I was not a Communist, cynical rivalry had put me in charge of one of the Party's leading cultural organizations" (68).

Wright's need for literary recognition and support also influenced his decision to join the Party. He began his career as a revolutionary poet in the Reed Club, turning out fairly standard proletarian calls for unity among workers and glimpses of the communist utopia. His sixteen so-called "radical" poems move from a dogmatic militancy to a more restrained faith in the Marxist solution to world problems (Fabre, *Quest* 99). His desire to have some control over *Left Front*, the magazine that printed his poetry, figured in his accepting the position in the club. Fabre concludes that "although he did admire the Party's fight for racial equality, it seems that Wright's motives for joining were more literary than political" (*Quest* 103). In 1933 the Party singled out Wright as a model proletarian artist and exerted pressure on him to become an official member. Wright set a condition regarding artistic freedom which would become the focal point of his subsequent friction with the Party: "I was informed that if I wanted to continue as secretary of the club I would have to join the Communist Party. I stated that I favored a policy that allowed for the development of writers and artists. My policy was accepted. I signed the membership card" (*Hunger* 69). Thus began Wright's official relationship with the Communist Party, which would last more than ten years and would provide him with a sense of home or security until he would strike out on his own again. Wright would use a Marxist and communist framework for his literary productions from 1934 through 1941. By 1942 his private disillusionment with the Party would become well-known, and he would formally sever his connection in 1944 (Brignano 52).

From the very beginning of Wright's association with the Party, however, he felt that its discipline was rather arbitrary and its vision of life too narrow for his needs as a creative writer. Even his first hopeful intentions, recalled later in his essay "I Tried to Be a Communist," support these feelings:

> The Communists, I felt, had oversimplified the experience of
> those whom they sought to lead. In their efforts to recruit masses,
> they had missed the meaning of the *lives* of the masses, had
> conceived of people in too abstract a manner. I would try to put
> some of that meaning back. I would tell Communists how
> common people felt, and I would tell common people of the self-
> sacrifice of Communists who strove for unity among them.
> (Kinnamon 53)

In the same essay Wright argued from his own early experience that the
opportunistic party leadership used artists and intellectuals only as suppliers of
propaganda. Wright opposed Party interference in his mission as a writer and
resisted its orders to perform what he saw as essentially menial tasks. He
comments in *American Hunger* on his superior's instructions that he organize
a committee against the high cost of living: "I was in the midst of writing a novel
and he was calling me to tabulate the price of groceries" (105). Fabre explains
that for Wright

> the dilemma was insoluble; either he would have to conform to the
> party directives and thus sacrifice his integrity as a writer, or he
> would once again be cut off and isolated. For the time being, he
> tried to stall, in order to remain part of the cultural organizations
> of the Left and without becoming a mere political tool. (107)

In a letter to his editor in 1959 Wright described an early break from, and then
re-entry into the Party:

> The American Communist Party tried strenuously to convince me
> that writing was not my forte and that I would serve better as an
> organizer. I refused to accept this and withdrew from the Commu-
> nist Party. Feeling that the Communist Party in New York was
> more liberal and intelligent, I left Chicago for New York in 1936,
> and upon arrival, I was reinstated into the Communist Party and
> given charge of the Harlem Bureau of the *Daily Worker*. (Fabre,
> *Quest* 138)

His "Blueprint for Negro Writing" (1937), an attempt to reconcile Marxism and black nationalism, could not conceal his concern about the inartistic didacticism virtually required of the artist by Marxist theory:

> For the Negro writer, Marxism is but the starting point. No theory of life can take the place of life. After Marxism has laid bare the skeleton of society, there remains the task of the writer to plant flesh upon those bones out of his will to live. . . . If the sensory vehicle of imaginative writing is required to carry too great a load of didactic material, the artistic sense is submerged. (Kinnamon 71)

This statement proves ironic especially when applied to Wright's most successful novel, *Native Son*, which sacrifices some of its artistic integrity because of too much didactic material. As Wright summed up his objection to the Party's placing the needs of society above the immediate need of the individual, "I wanted to be a Communist, but my kind of Communist. I wanted to shape people's feelings, awaken their hearts" (Brignano 52). One senses Wright's contained but growing dissatisfaction with the Party's response to racial problems in a letter of 1940:

> I do not agree with Ben Davis when he implies that the majority of the Negroes are with the labor movement. . . . My aim in depicting Jan was to show that even for that great Party which has thrown down a challenge to America on the Negro question such as no other party, there is much, much to do, and, above all, to understand. (Fabre, *Quest* 186)

In spite of his fidelity to the problems of blacks, Wright encountered cold treatment from other black communists for his interest in writing:

> They commented upon my shined shoes, my clean shirt. Above all, my manner of speech had seemed an alien thing to them. . . . I found that they were not vicious, they had no intention to hurt. They just did not know anything and did not want to learn anything. . . . The word "writer" was enough to make a black Chicago Communist feel that the men to whom the word applied had gone wrong. (*Hunger* 77)

White communists, too, regarded Wright with distrust for his individualism and supposed intellectuality:

> The irony of it was that I, who had all but to steal books to read, had been branded as an intellectual by the one group that claimed it was dedicated to educating the oppressed and informing them with a vision of life. . . . I had expressed no opinion regarding the leadership of the party or its work. But the rumors of my dissatisfaction persisted. (*Hunger* 87)

The discovery that one of two communist leaders fighting for control was a mental patient provided Wright with a natural metaphor for his feelings about the party: "I was thunderstruck. Was this true? Undoubtedly it was. Then what kind of club did we run that a lunatic could step into it and help run it? Were we all so mad that we could not detect a madman when we saw one?" (73). He felt that "an invisible wall was building between me and the people with whom I had cast my lot" (78).

Much of Wright's fiction and nonfiction of the 1930s and early 1940s represents his attempt to weld Marxist social analysis onto deterministic naturalism, which had been his formative literary influence. Of the more recent specialists in American literary naturalism, only Donald Pizer even mentions Wright, dismissing *Native Son* from his study on the grounds that it is seriously flawed. Notwithstanding this lack of critical attention, *Uncle Tom's Children* and *Native Son* show the clear influence of both European and American naturalism. In Wright's introduction to *Native Son* he paraphrases Zola's pseudo-scientific approach for arriving at truth in fiction. Wright's early work shares naturalism's most common theme of the waste of individual potential because of the forces of environment and heredity (Pizer 6). Many readers and critics of naturalism have found fault with its evident vacillation and inconsistency between determinism and free will, its mixing of fate and moral responsibility. While this issue is taken up specifically with regard to Wright's work below, the defenders of naturalism hold that the opposing attitudes of

hope and despair establish a creative tension between determinism and re-
formism. Charles Walcutt finds that the naturalist's "unspoken ideal" makes
the reader "aware of the opposition between what the artist says about man's
fate and what his saying it affirms about man's hope" (29).

The union of naturalism and Marxism would seem a compatible one, for
both theories tend to argue a maximum of forces beyond the individual's
control and a minimum of free will. Although the ideology of Marxism offers
more hope for social change than does bleak literary naturalism, it remains
rooted in materialistic determinism, which might be said to belie or contradict
that hope. Marxism seemed to offer Wright an opportunity to retain the basic
tenets of his accustomed naturalism and still look ahead (though somewhat
contradictorily) to the transformation of the world--the difference, it would
appear, lying in collective rather than in individual action. Marxism gave
Wright a means of tempering his anger over the persecution of blacks in
America with the belief that whites themselves (dominating the numbers of the
Communist party) would lead the way toward harmony. But, aside from the
problem of contradiction in the Marxist fusion of freedom and necessity, the
adaptation of Marxist materials to naturalistic fiction in Wright's case often
resulted in clumsy, didactic intrusions on narrative and character and in visions
of the glorious future not sustained by the grim present.

The second weakness of Wright's "literary Marxism," one not so much
literary as ideological, and evident especially in *Uncle Tom's Children*, is that
the sloganeering and white-led activism is superseded by a sense of black
nationalism which betrays a more individualized source of hope than is
sanctioned by collective Marxism. (This sense of black nationalism diverted
Ellison more quickly than Wright from the attractions of communism.) One
senses that Wright's literary problem may have been caused partly by his
growing impatience with communist authoritarianism and may have been a
reflection of his repressed opposition to the Communist Party. This mixture of
attitudes, suggesting his more fundamental loyalty to worldwide black

nationalism than to communism, can also be found in his early nonfiction works "Blueprint for Negro Writing" (1937) and *12 Million Black Voices* (1941). Ironically, the greatest intrusion of Marxist propaganda occurs in *Native Son*, which also presents implicit but strong criticism of the Party as often racist and insincere toward blacks, a theme which would become explicit in *The Outsider* as well as in Ellison's *Invisible Man*.

Wright decided not to publish his first novel, *Lawd Today*, written probably in 1936 (and published posthumously in 1963), because it would have intensified his already somewhat strained relationship with the Party. His unsympathetic treatment of his lower-middle class protagonist would not have appealed to party aestheticians, who expected dynamic heroes representing the oppressed proletariat. The heavily naturalistic tone of the novel offers no relief from the depressing depiction of Jake, the defeated protagonist. Margolies suggests that Wright's decision not to publish it had obvious reasons:

> His relationship to the party intelligentsia, already sensitive, would have been considerably exacerbated. Yet Wright's decision to keep the manuscript, despite his knowledge that the party would have disapproved, arouses the suspicion that notwithstanding his dedication to the party, somewhere in the back of his mind he foresaw the possibility of leaving the party and using the story. (92)

Several years after his break with the Party, Wright transformed several parts of *Lawd Today* into his existentialist *The Outsider,* in which rebellion against destiny or fate becomes nihilistic but demonstrates not the burden of determinism but the burden of freedom.

The short stories collected in *Uncle Tom's Children* exhibit a counterpoint between, on one hand, deterministic and materialistic forces obstructing human freedom and, on the other, their characters' instinctive longing for freedom, which finds expression in their progressively increasing resistance to their hostile environment. Fabre points out that "each protagonist is more committed to the social struggle than the last, more responsible and hence more victorious because he acts less from purely personal motives'' (*Quest* 161). Brignano finds a "novel-like development in the arrangement of Marxist undertones until at last, personal fulfillment and social salvation are identified with action and hope in the Communist Party" (Brignano 61). The first three stories implicitly establish the need for communism without explicit mention of it by depicting the dreadful conditions in which blacks are forced to commit violence in order to save their lives; the last two stories posit the hope that communism can effect an amelioration of the horrors of black life in America and can lead to racial harmony. Margolies praises *Uncle Tom's Children* for avoiding explicit Marxist didacticism (58), and Kinnamon finds it happily lacking "the homiletic essays placed in the mouths of characters in *Native Son* and *The Outsider*" (108). Those assessments have validity at least for the first three stories, which present the typical Wrightian theme of a young black man's initiation into violence as a means of survival and of realizing identity. Wright's depiction of violence in *Uncle Tom's Children*, however, argues two possibly conflicting motivations, which correspond to his materialistic Marxism and his evolving belief in personality. On one hand, he offers the environmental necessity of the killing in self-defense in "Big Boy Leaves Home" and "Down by the Riverside"; on the other, he suggests the existential need for the individual's expression of personality, even if (as in *The House of the Dead* and *Notes from Underground*) that expression is perverse and self-destructive. In both these stories, Wright shows black violence as virtually unavoidable, as a justified or understandable response to white violence and hatred. In *Native Son* and *The Outsider*, on the other hand, murder becomes an experiment in self-will and self-definition, a groping for some kind of responsibility if only to oneself over against all others.

These stories' assertions of personality and human dignity, even in death, tend to compete with and undermine their deterministic framework. In "Big Boy Leaves Home" Wright establishes the motif of self-defense with the title character's plainly justified killing of the white man who has already killed two black boys; Big Boy's escape and survival mark him as more fortunate than most of Wright's protagonists, who usually meet violent death themselves. Mann of "Down by the Riverside" also kills to save himself from a direct and deadly white threat. His death, like that of Silas in "Long Black Song" and of Sue in "Bright and Morning Star," is a last demand for dignity and a defiant assertion of individual worth. Mann's refusal to die "by the rules" at the hands of racist soldiers is paralleled by Silas's courageous if desperate death inside the burning house and Sue's free choice to accept death from the sheriff's men after executing her son's betrayer. Sue's words upon dying typify the attitude of the other two protagonists as well: "Yuh didnt git what yuh wanted! N yuh ain gonna git it! Yuh didnt kill me; Ah come here by mahsef" (215). Both Silas's and Sue's killing whites involves not self-defense but rather outrage over violations of their dignity, his reason being the seduction of his wife by a white man and hers the torture of her son.

Although the inclusion of Marxist materials and themes in *Uncle Tom's Children* is not nearly as artistically heavy-handed as later in *Native Son*, its explicit use in the two concluding stories, "Fire and Cloud" and "Bright and Morning Star," is somewhat forced. It is also overshadowed by their characters' black nationalism. Both stories depict a black character's conversion from traditional Christianity, associated by Wright with passivity and social inaction, to radical social activism through the Communist Party. Reverend Taylor of "Fire and Cloud" embodies the movement of the first three stories toward social rather than individual resistance. However, Wright's idealistic but not very convincing vision of blacks and whites marching together seems a vague and rather implausible means to a more just economic system. Taylor's new zeal for collective radical action sounds simply like communist sloganeering in a black dialect: "We gotta git wid the people, son" (171). A similar didactic heaviness of hand affects "Bright and Morning Star," in which Wright attempts the conversion of Sue to militant collectivism as the modern successor of her cherished Christianity. "Bright and Morning Star" approaches what Brignano calls "sheer propaganda" (132) with its obligatory depiction of blacks and whites uniting to combat injustice. Both this story and "Fire and Cloud" feature white characters who are not hostile to blacks, but in Brignano's estimation "they are merely cardboard figures, just as unreal and invisible as the white people in *Black Boy*" (19). Sue's sacrificial death at the conclusion of "Bright and Morning Star" is quite convincing artistically, but the strength of her black nationalist motivation ironically tends to weaken the explicit endorsement of communism for which Wright prepares throughout *Uncle Tom's Children*. As Margolies argues,

> Taylor and Sue arrive at their decisions as a result of their peculiar Negro folk mysticism--or, perhaps, as Wright would have it, a native Negro revolutionism. Even Sue is a Negro first, before she is a Communist. . . . Wright's militant Negroes, despite their protestations to the contrary, often sound more like black nationalists than Communist internationalists. It was perhaps this facet of Wright's work, in addition to the obvious, extreme, and frequent isolated individualism of his heroes that had begun to disturb Communist party officials. (72)

Fabre adds that "Wright's vacillation between the ethnic and Marxist perspectives certainly reflects Wright's own ambivalence at the time of composition in spite of his firm propagandistic intentions" (*Quest* 164). Wright's portrayal of white treachery toward blacks even within the Communist Party suggests a root distrust of white benevolence and evolves into the much stronger criticism of communism in *Native Son* and *The Outsider*. Nevertheless, the favorable reception of *Uncle Tom's Children* in 1937 made Wright for the time being one of the literary stars of the party.

Two of Wright's early nonfiction works, "Blueprint for Negro Writing" and *12 Million Black Voices*, also reflect his struggle to reconcile Marxist materialism and his emerging awareness of blacks' need to create values and to assert personality. Exploring in "Blueprint for Negro Writing" the relationship between literature and politics, Wright called for an end to black writers' isolation and a collective effort among black writers as well as between black and white writers. Yet he scolded the Harlem Renaissance writers for their "pandering" to a white audience and ignoring the needs of blacks, and urged the assimilation of black folklore into a literary sensibility informed by the Marxist view of society (Kinnamon 71). Wright's view that one's "Marxist analysis of society. . . should unify his personality" ("Blueprint" 44) plainly ignores the anti-metaphysical thrust of Marxism. His statement that the black writer must "create values by which his race is to struggle, live, and die" (43) sounds un-materialistic and, from the communist point of view, dangerously individual-istic. His hope for a literary vision embodying "a complex simplicity, to borrow a phrase from the Russians," (45) would seem to denigrate the preaching and didacticism inherent in Marxist propagandizing and also present to a degree in Wright's own work of this period. *12 Million Black Voices*, ostensibly a Marxist analysis of black American history, is much more a folk history blended with Wright's personal reaction to his southern and then his northern urban environ-ment. Described not as a scholarly study but as a "prose-poem account of the lives of simple folk in their own voices" (Margolies 23), this work sounds the subjective theme of race rather than the objective, Marxist one of class. It reflects the dominance of Wright's emotional protest against injustice over his superimposed, "rational" Marxist dialectic (Brignano 71).

Although Wright was officially affiliated with the Communist Party for more than ten years, by seven or eight years after joining in 1933 he began to recognize the inevitability of a split. His final year of intensive Party activity was 1941, and in 1942 he ceased his usual endorsement of Party causes. While planning a Party conference of left-wing writers, Wright suggested that they deal with craft problems, but he was overruled in favor of political questions. Subsequently, unfounded rumors began that he was a dangerous enemy of the Party and that he was organizing a secret opposition group (*Hunger* 90). Wright remained committed to his mission as an artist and began to avoid Party members:

> The artist and the politician stand at opposite poles. The artist enhances life by his prolonged concentration upon it, while the politician emphasizes the impersonal aspect of life by his attempts to fit men into groups.... The politician, eager to do good for men, may sneer at the artist because the art product cannot be used by him.... My writing was my way of seeing, my way of living, my way of feeling. My relationship with Communists reached a static phase. I shunned them and they shunned me. (93)

After Wright had written an article in 1942 titled "Not My People's War," skeptical of the fruits of black involvement in World War II, the Communist Party pressured him into changing it into an appeal for blacks to volunteer for service. This incident left Wright with an extreme distaste for Party discipline, and it marked the end of his submission to arbitrary autocratic control. A few months later, he refused several requests that he give a lecture for the Party. In his last words in a Party publication he implicitly rejected authoritarian Party control and called for "multiple points of view, expressed from varied environmental class angles" (Kinnamon 155). In *American Hunger* Wright relates feeling discouraged and angry with the Party when some white Communists at a congress balked at helping a black Communist find lodging for the night: "The problem of the clubs did not seem important. What did seem important was: Could a Negro ever live halfway like a human being in this goddam country?" (97). He describes his feelings upon making his decision to leave the Party:

> When I awakened next day, I did not want to go to the congress. I lay in bed thinking: I've got to go it alone. I've got to learn how again.... I decided that my relationship with the Party was about over; I would have to leave it.... Again I resolved to leave the Party, for the emotional cost of membership was too high. (99)

The decision was especially difficult because Wright had to abandon with the Party the best source of community he had found. Yet when he learned that the party would not support a court fight against government discrimination, he withdrew from it quietly, not making a public declaration for several months

(Fabre, *Quest* 299).

After his break with the Party, Wright retained something of his Marxist perspective, but he became a stronger proponent than ever of the autonomy and freedom of the individual. Having rejected the American Communist Party for its lack of attention to racism and to the development of the individual, he continued to believe in a socialist upheaval of society (Fabre, *Quest* 231). Even though he fought communism himself for the rest of his life, other Western opponents of communism disapproved of Wright because he did not relinquish his socialist views. In a letter he wrote:

> I lift my hand to fight Communism and I find that the hand of the Western world is sticking knives into my back. That is a crazy position. The Western world must make up its mind as to whether it hates Communists more than it hates colored people. It cannot, without being foolish, act as though it hates both people equally. (Fabre, *Quest* 517)

In another letter he elaborated upon his attitude toward the Party:

> In short, when I was a member of the Communist Party, I took that party seriously, and when I discovered that I was holding a tainted instrument in my hands, I dropped that instrument.... I felt a kind of grim exhilaration in facing a world in which nothing could be taken for granted, a world in which one had to create and forge one's meaning for one's own self. (Fabre, *Quest* 230)

As he was planning the first volume of his autobiography, *Black Boy,* he wrote, "The book will really be an expression of my own spiritual hunger. I had once thought that Communism was an instrument for that, but now I don't know. They beat you down too much with dictatorial methods of work and feeling and thought" (Fabre, *Quest* 273). One finds the same focus on individuality in the second volume, *American Hunger*: "I was branded a traitor, an unstable personality, and one whose faith had failed. . . . They had never been able to conquer their fear of the individual way in which I had acted and lived, an individuality which life had seared into my blood and bones" (112).

Significantly enough, the Party's denial of Wright's freedom as an artist had opened his eyes to their underlying denial of human individuality:

> Writing had to be done in loneliness, and Communism had declared war upon human loneliness. Alone, they said, a man was weak; united with others, he was strong. Therefore they habitually feared a man who stood alone.... The Communism I looked upon was impatient of extended processes, of results that could not be obtained overnight, of an act that could not be performed in a day. This was how America had embraced Communism: this was America's first fruit of materialistic rebellion. (*Hunger* 123)

In his 1945 essay "The God That Failed," Wright criticized both radicals and conservatives for their attempts to objectify and manipulate blacks: "Both the political Left and the political Right try to change the Negro problem into something that they can control, thereby denying the humanity of the Negro, excluding his unique and historic position in American life" (Brignano 83). And in an introduction to George Padmore's *Pan-Africanism or Communism*, Wright sums up his period of communist involvement and his personalist objections:

> The Negro's fundamental loyalty is, therefore, to *himself*. His situation makes this inevitable. . . . The Negro, even when embracing Communism or Western Democracy, is not supporting ideologies: he is seeking to use *instruments* (instruments owned and controlled by men of other races!) for his own ends. He stands outside of those instruments and ideologies; he has to do so, for he is not allowed to blend with them in a natural, organic, and healthy manner. (Neal 60)

The Communist Party's refusal to acknowledge the individual and the artist in Wright only intensified his personalist commitment. This development was paralleled, generally and less dramatically, in the experience of Ellison.

IV

In an essay published in 1957 titled "Society, Morals, and the Novel," Ralph Ellison describes his idea of the novelist's duty "to give the reader that which we do have in abundance: all the countless untold and wonderful variations on the themes of identity and freedom and necessity, love and death . . . all the mystery of personality undergoing its endless metamorphosis" (91). But this emphasis on personality had to evolve in Ellison, just as it did in Wright, away from a determinism-tinged naturalism and a literary apprentice-ship in the shadow of the Communist Party. Although Ellison never became a Party member, the influence of its ideas on him can be estimated by the force and number of his later statements refuting materialistic collectivism and the literary implications of Marxist theory. The 1930s and early 1940s mark Ellison's period of immersion in radical politics, when he wrote short stories, essays, and reviews attuned to Marxism and confronting the social issues of the time. In his book of essays *Shadow and Act* (1964) Ellison has little to say about details of his Marxist commitment, but he does note that his "boyish ideal" of measuring up to certain standards "served to mock and caution me when I became interested in the communist ideal" (xvii). He adds that he was forced to a new awareness "through my struggles with the craft of fiction; yes, and by my attraction (soon rejected) to Marxist political theory, which was my response to the inferior status which society sought to impose upon me" (xxi). After meeting Wright in 1936, Ellison was introduced to the orbit of the Communist Party, frequently thereafter attending Party political gatherings. Yet Ellison would later minimize Wright's role in his radical formation:

> I did not need Wright to tell me how to be a Negro, or how to be angry or to express anger, or even to teach me about socialism; my mother had canvassed for the socialists, not the communists, the year I was born. No, I had been a Negro for twenty-two or twenty-three years when I met Wright, and in more places and under a

greater variety of circumstances than he had then known. (141)

Ellison's remaining outside the Communist Party can probably be ascribed both to his individualism and to his considerable suspicions about the party from the start. Those suspicions extended to the legitimacy of proletarian fiction, as Ellison noted in an interview: "I was seeking to learn, and social realism was a highly regarded theory, even though I didn't think too much of the so-called proletarian fiction even when I was most impressed by Marxism" ("Art" 39).

Although both communist ideology and naturalism colored Ellison's polemical essays and fiction of the late thirties and early forties, his rather rapid evolution toward a more individual-oriented and a more affirmative vision indicated a break with his formative influences. According to Marxist theory, literature becomes propaganda when it enters the social sphere; the revolutionary writer's duty is to sharpen the class consciousness of the proletariat to prepare them for overthrowing the ruling classes and seizing the means of production (Neal 59). Between 1937 and 1944 Ellison wrote more than twenty essays and reviews for several leftist periodicals, often reflecting, as O'Meally notes, an explicitly Marxist viewpoint:

> Ellison's criticism often described black Americans as citizens of a state or nation (like a Russian soviet) within the U.S. The literature of black Americans was, Ellison believed, an emerging national literature that should serve to heighten the revolutionary consciousness of the black populace. The black writer should not instill in his audience mere "race consciousness," however, but awareness of class. Ideally the revolutionary black writer inspired black working people to unite with workers of other "nationalities" against the bourgeoisie, white and black. On the whole, black writers had failed in their revolutionary calling. (38)

In "The Way It Is," published in *New Masses* in 1942, Ellison described the suffering in Harlem while the war was being fought by a Jim Crow army. "An American Dilemma" (1944) and "Harlem is Nowhere" (1948) also dealt in radical terms with, respectively, the involvement of black politics with philanthropic big business and the effects of Harlem misery on its residents. But in Ellison's emphasis on political and social relevancy one senses what O'Meally calls

> another kind of spirit trying to cut through the Marxist phrase-mongering, another kind of spirit trying to develop a less simplistic, more viable attitude toward not only the usable content of Afro-American culture in America, but more importantly, a sense of the *meaning* of that culture's presence and its manifestations as they impinged upon ''white culture.'' (44)

Ellison at first modeled his criticism and fiction on that of Wright. His essays "Richard Wright and Negro Fiction" (1941) and "Stormy Weather" (1940) work the Marxist vein of Wright's "Blueprint for Negro Writing," the former praising *Uncle Tom's Children* both as literature and as a radical political statement. For the time being Ellison championed the realism and photographic clarity of Steinbeck and Wright, though later he would directly repudiate "journalistic" fiction. He saw the black writer's function both as inspiring his people to overcome the difficulties of survival in a racist society and as creating, in his words, ''the consciousness of his oppressed nation'' (O'Meally 40).

One observes early in Ellison's career as a writer of fiction the development of a vision too complex and paradoxical for the narrow bounds of Marxism and naturalism. One also notes his growing appreciation of black traditions and folklore as a personalist alternative to materialistic radicalism. Of his attempts to transcend protest he commented, ''I wrote what might be called propaganda--having to do with the Negro struggle--but my fiction was always trying to be something else: something different even from Wright's fiction. I never accepted the ideology which the *New Masses* attempted to impose on writers'' (Neal 64). In a 1967 interview titled "A Very Stern Discipline," Ellison remarked, "If you'll note--and the record is public--I never wrote the official type of fiction'' (86). In the early 1940s Ellison seems to have gone beyond the view that literature must make a radical political statement, to an understanding that artistic vision transcends polemicizing. He eventually came to assert the writer's need and moral duty to remain open to the complexity and even contrariety of experience:

> The ideology changes, but the human experience, the joy and the pain, the anger and the exultation which should go into art remains. . . . It isn't yours; it's a group thing which you share in and which you communicate. . . . If you *do* that, then it seems a far more important thing than being ideologically committed. The novel is a form which attempts to deal with the contradictions of life and ambivalence and ambiguities of values. It isn't easy for ideologies to deal with it. They don't trust it because the form itself insists upon a certain kind of truth, a certain kind of objectivity. (O'Meally 4)

Attention to problems of craft helped Ellison to realize that the truly revolutionary work of art is that which is well-made and which faithfully pictures life. In "Richard Wright and Negro Fiction" he observed that serious writers "know that the safety of American culture depends as much upon the spread of their craft knowledge as upon the growth of trade unions and other organizations of social struggle" (13). Ellison often has advised writers to hone their mastery of technique and to avoid the pitfall of black stereotypes (O'Meally 41).

Ellison's first two stories, "Slick Gonna Learn" (1939) and "The Birthmark" (1940), offer a straightforward naturalism blended with exhortations for blacks to join leftist political organizations to fight injustice. "Slick," set in the naturalistic mold of Dreiser and Wright, shows its protagonist, Slick Williams, as all but defeated by the extremely racist and oppressive white environment. Surprisingly released by a judge after striking a policeman, Slick is beaten and almost killed by a group of policemen who then leave to quell a riot of striking workers at a plant. With this story Ellison attempts to demonstrate the importance of blacks' viewing their situation not just in a racial context but in terms of the revolution of all workers, black and white. The white trucker's compassionate assistance to Slick at the story's conclusion suggests that the individual's task is to realize his solidarity with all other workers. "The Birthmark," also depicting the viciousness of life in the South, poses the question of how one should react to incidents like the lynching and castration of the protagonist Matt's brother Willie. The white lawmen transparently lie that Willie was killed in an automobile accident, and the only response which will save Matt's and his sister's lives is submission to the official prevarication. Ellison again implies that outrage must be channeled into productive (i.e., radical) political action.

Yet the prevailing darkness of naturalism, even with the element of hope provided by militant collectivism, did not suit Ellison for long. He became dissatisfied with the defeatism of the typical naturalistic story, in which impersonal forces overwhelm the individual:

> As early as 1940, Ellison found himself increasingly unwilling to portray the black American as the spirit-broken product of the outside forces set against him. He was beginning to envisage black characters who were able to understand their environment and to master it by positive action or by the magic of art. By 1940 too, Ellison realized that his view of fiction was quite different from that of Wright and other realists. His concern with the strengths of the black character, with style, with folklore, and with history as a "repository of values" eclipsed his enchantment with black proletarians, scarred, battered, on the run. (O'Meally 38)

At the same time, Ellison's political tracts were shifting their focus from the environment to the individual's ability to survive his difficult circumstances. And Ellison's desire for conscious protagonists, quite possibly related to his study of the nineteenth-century Russians' need to improve upon their superfluous men, seems to have contributed to the implicit anti-naturalism of his next three stories.

In "Afternoon" (1940), "Mister Toussan" (1941), and "That I Had the Wings" (1943), two ten-year-old black boys, Buster and Riley, are emboldened to assert themselves in a spirit of confidence against their environment by their assimilation of black folklore. With "Afternoon" Ellison drops the political and ideological baggage of the previous stories, and shows how the boys' identification with folk heroes inspires them with the possibility of becoming victors themselves (O'Meally 62). "Mister Toussan" also stands as criticism of the naturalists' dismissal of folklore, for here the boys emulate "Sweet Papa Toussan" of the Haitian revolution and are moved to action against an unjust societal restriction. Buster and Riley transform Ole Bill the rooster into a folk hero in "That I Had the Wings"; they gain a sense of power from their use of folk rhymes and from their attempt to defy the limitations of their barnyard animals. These stories illustrate the evolution of Ellison's central theme of "the bursting forth of Negro personality form the fixed boundaries of Southern life" and the "journeying forth of the soul" epitomized in American transcendentalism (Bone 28). Even in "Stormy Weather," a somewhat radical essay published in 1940, Ellison had begun this emphasis on folklore, claiming that the black writer must recognize that "the spread of this consciousness, added to the passion and sensitivity of the Negro people . . . will help create a new way of life in the United States" (O'Meally 43). Most of Ellison's subsequent work, and especially *Invisible Man*, shows folk traditions and values as the key to blacks' self-awareness and strength to overcome their environment.

Ellison's three stories published in 1944, "In a Strange Land," "Flying Home," and "King of the Bingo Game," further show his evolution from naturalism and narrow political activism toward his mature exploration of the personalist themes of self-identity, possibility, and responsibility for creating one's own meanings. The protagonist of "In a Strange Land," Parker, a black man familiar with Shakespeare and Russian folk music, finds his situation as a black GI overseas dangerous, for the white American soldiers respond to his presence with a severe beating. Parker finds his escape from such hostility and confusion in a new sense of identity gained from hearing the American national anthem and realizing that his own love of jazz unifies him with American ideals, no matter how tarnished they may become in some people. With "Flying Home" Ellison offers another protagonist who learns to transcend and to overcome his brutal environment through the discovery of the wisdom and strength of his black American traditions. Todd, the black airman in training, has his only sense of freedom when in the air, suspended between racist whites and poor Alabama blacks, of whom he is ashamed. Through Todd's attention to the folk tale related by old Jefferson, an illiterate black man who helps him after his plane has crashed, he avoids being killed by the racist landowner Graves. Like the later protagonist of *Invisible Man*, Todd reverses his opinion on the viability of black folk values, and this decision saves his life and directs him toward a future of rich potential. "King of the Bingo Game," usually considered an apt thematic and artistic prelude to *Invisible Man*, exhibits Ellison's mature surrealist or antirealist voice and introduces the elements of the individual's dizzying freedom and his power to control his fate. Here the protagonist is not especially nourished by any memories of southern folk culture, and he must rely on his personal creativity to forge his identity. His refusal to play the bingo game by its established rules leads to his awakening. Ellison's anti-naturalistic tone in these three stories is summed up in a statement in *Shadow and Act*: "Literature teaches us that mankind has always defined itself against the negatives thrown it by both society and the universe. It is the human will, human hope, and human effort which makes the difference" (49). In 1944, the same year these stories were published, Ellison began the seven-year task of writing *Invisible Man*, which would be his ultimate refutation of naturalism and materialistic collectivism.

Ellison's support of the American Communist Party waned and dissolved in the early 1940s, and he became a critic of the materialism of leftist movements. Already critical of some aspects of left-wing politics, Ellison, together with many other blacks of similar political persuasions, was deeply disgusted with the Party's support in 1944 of the segregated U.S. armed forces. The Party's indifference to the "little Hitlers," Ellison's term for white

American racists who oppressed blacks at home, also drove him to renounce his unofficial support of it (O'Meally 54). He asserted the exploitative nature of the Party and warned blacks about becoming involved:

> They fostered the myth that Communism was twentieth-century Americanism, but to be a twentieth-century American meant, in their thinking, that you had to be more Russian than American and less Negro than either. That's how they lost the Negroes. The Communists recognized no plurality of interests and were really responding to the necessities of Soviet foreign policy and when the war came, Negroes got caught and were made expedient in the shifting of policy. Just as Negroes who fool around with them to-day are going to get caught in the next turn of the screw. (Neal 61)

In *Shadow and Act* he objected to the left's materialistic denial of blacks' humanity, and he equated that denial with the underlying cynicism of the New Deal:

> Both, it might be said, went about solving the Negro problem without defining the nature of the problem beyond its economic and narrowly political aspects. Which is not unusual for politi-cians--only here both groups consistently professed and demon-strated far more social vision than the average political party. . . . It would be easy . . . to question the sincerity of these two groups. . . . But this would be silly. Sincerity is not a quality that one expects of political parties, not even revolutionary ones. . . . Regardless of their long-range intentions, on the practical level parties are not guided by humanism so much as by the expedien-cies of power. (310)

In the 1950s Ellison continued to criticize the left and declared that certain kinds of literary realism reveal "everything except the nature of man" (O'Meally 38). He did continue to align himself with the social struggle of blacks in America, joining and supporting the NAACP and admiring the courage of Martin Luther King. Yet he also continued to affirm that "literature draws upon much deeper and much more slowly changing centers of the human personality than does politics" ("Discipline" 86). As the civil rights movement developed,

72

he expressed confidence that activist blacks understood his commitment: "I assure you that no Negroes are beating down my door, putting pressure on me to join the Negro Freedom Movement, for the simple reason that they realize that I am enlisted for the duration" (*Shadow* 142).

In the years since his break with naturalism and proletarian fiction, Ellison has made many statements of his ideological and aesthetic rationale. He has high praise for Wright's attempt to return the novel to its "impelling moral function" (*Shadow* 164) and for his converting "the American Negro impulse toward self-annihilation and 'going underground' into a will to confront the world, to evaluate his experience honestly and throw his findings unashamedly into the guilty conscience of America" (*Shadow* 212). But Ellison also frankly notes the demarcation between Wright and himself that proceeds from their different views on "ideological art," aesthetics, and determinism. Ellison discusses some of his basic differences with Wright:

> I think I felt more complexity in life, and my background made me aware of a larger area of possibility. . . . Also, I think I was less interested in an ideological interpretation of Negro experience. . . .
> When I came to discover a little more about what I wanted to express, I felt that Wright was overcommitted to ideology--even though I, too, wanted many of the same things for our people. You might say that I was much less a social determinist. But I suppose that basically it comes down to a difference in our concepts of the individual. (*Shadow* 16)

He confides his early problems with Wright's ideological view of art:

> Wright believed in the much abused idea that novels are "weapons"--the counterpart of the dreary notion, common among most minority groups, that novels are instruments of good public relations. But I believe that true novels, even when most pessimistic and bitter, arise out of an impulse to celebrate human life and therefore are ritualistic and ceremonial at their core. Thus they would preserve as they destroy, affirm as they reject. . . .
> I felt no need to attack what I considered the limitations of his vision because I was quite impressed by what he had achieved. . . .

> Still I would write my own books, and they would be in them-
> selves, implicitly, criticisms of Wright's. . . .
>
> How awful that Wright found the facile answers of Marxism
> before he learned to use literature as a means of discovering the
> forms of American Negro humanity. (*Shadow* 117)

Ellison neglects to mention, however, Wright's evolution away from ideology
and the protest novel and toward the existentialism of "The Man Who Lived
Underground" and *The Outsider*. In fact, *The Outsider*, published only months
after *Invisible Man*, parallels Ellison's novel in its rejection of communism for
offenses against human freedom and in its elevation of creative revolt and
choice of self for personal fulfillment.

Although for a time Ellison had denigrated Hemingway for his inattention
to ideology in his novels, later he chose Hemingway over Wright for precisely
this reason, and for Hemingway's rejection of defeatism:

> Do you still ask why Hemingway was more important to me than
> Wright? . . . Because he knew the difference between politics and
> art and something of their true relationship for the writer. Because
> all that he wrote was imbued with a spirit beyond the tragic with
> which I could feel at home, for it was very close to the feeling of
> the blues. (*Shadow* 140)

On the other hand, Ellison recognized Wright's debt to Dostoevsky, especially
in *Black Boy's* recalling *The House of the Dead* as a "psychological document
of life under oppressive conditions" (*Shadow* 201). In his early comments on
Black Boy (in "Black Boy's Blues") Ellison tended to defend Wright's strong
emphasis on environment. Later, when Ellison had broken fully from Wright's
influence and had formulated explicitly his anti-naturalism, he argued that
Wright's accent on environment over the individual's power to overcome was
"doubtlessly . . . the beginning of Wright's exile" (*Shadow* 126). In a reversal
of his early emulation of the naturalists' journalistic methods, he wrote, "The
naturalists stick to case histories and sociology and are willing to compete with
the camera and the tape recorder. I despise concreteness in writing" (*Shadow*
180).

Although Ellison tends to minimize the problem of incorporating protest within a work of fictional art, he places his rejection of naturalism and of ideological battles in American literature's tradition of emphasizing fluidity and possibility. Poor attention to craft, he says, rather than protest per se, has been the undoing of many novels by blacks (*Shadow* 137). Ellison finds protest as an element of all art, "though it does not necessarily take the form of speaking for a political or social program. It might appear in a novel as a technical assault against the styles which have gone before, or as protest against the human condition" (*Shadow* 137). He goes so far as to recognize "no dichotomy between art and protest. Dostoevsky's *Notes from Underground* is, among other things, a protest against the limitations of nineteenth-century rationalism" (*Shadow* 169). Ellison deeply admires Melville and Twain for their moral concerns and for their taking "greater responsibility for the condition of democracy" (*Shadow* 104), as especially evident in *Moby Dick* and *Huckleberry Finn*. But he laments the American novel's abandonment after Twain of the "basic moral predicament" evident in the contradiction between our ideals and our social conduct: "Perhaps the discomfort about protest in books by Negro authors comes because since the nineteenth century American literature has avoided profound moral searching" (*Shadow* 183).

Thus the development of naturalism, in Ellison's view, was part of this avoidance in American literature of complex moral questions--not despite, but rather because of naturalism's oversimplified finger-pointing and its reluctance to posit personal responsibility. He therefore must reject naturalism as fundamentally un-American and undemocratic:

> Thus to see America with an awareness of its rich diversity and its almost magical fluidity and freedom, I was forced to conceive of a novel unburdened by the narrow naturalism which has led, after so many triumphs, to the final and unrelieved despair which marks so much of our current fiction. I was to dream of a prose which was flexible, and swift as American change is swift, confronting the inequalities and brutalities of our society forthrightly, but yet

thrusting forth its images of hope, human fraternity, and individual self-realization. (*Shadow* 105)

What Ellison seeks in the depiction of black America is, first, "that sensitively focused process of opposites, of good and evil, of instinct and intellect, of passion and spirituality, which the great literary art has projected as the image of man" (*Shadow* 26). Second, he insists upon affirming

those qualities which are of value beyond any question of segregation, economics, or previous condition of servitude.... What I have tried to commemorate in fiction is that which I believe to be enduring and abiding in our situation, especially those human qualities which the American Negro has developed despite and in rejection of the obstacles and meannesses imposed upon us. (*Shadow* 17, 21)

Ellison asks one criterion for his work, "that my fiction be judged as art; if it fails, it fails aesthetically, not because I did or did not fight some ideological battle" (*Shadow* 137). Looking back at the proletarian fiction of the 1930s and 1940s, he notices its occasional strengths, as in Malraux's *Man's Fate*, not in its political positions but in

its larger concern with the tragic struggle of humanity. Most of the social realists of the period were concerned less with tragedy than with injustice. I wasn't, and am not, primarily concerned with injustice, but with art....

It is through the process of making artistic forms, plays, poems, novels, out of one's experience that one becomes a writer, and it is through this process, this struggle, that the writer helps give meaning to the experience of the group.... If this sounds like an argument for the artist's withdrawal from social struggles, I would recall to you W. H. Auden's comment to the effect that "in our age, the mere making of a work of art is itself a political act." (*Shadow* 169, 147)

For Ellison, then, the individual's struggle to produce art, whatever isolation his task may impose on him, remains both radical and social.

Chapter 3

The Debate on Self-Will:
Crime and Punishment, *Native Son*, and *The Outsider*

I

The similarities between, and the evident influence of *Crime and Punishment* on *Native Son* and *The Outsider* have been referred to by a few critics, but none has performed any detailed analysis. Dasha Culic Nisula's "Dostoevsky and Richard Wright: From St. Petersburg to Chicago" sketches some general thematic and structural similarities between the works of Dostoevsky and Wright. Tony Magistrale in "From St. Petersburg to Chicago: Wright's *Crime and Punishment*" briefly examines the environmental parallels between *Native Son* and Dostoevsky's novel, but omits any treatment of the more numerous parallels with *The Outsider*. It seems that with his two major novels Wright consciously echoes *Crime and Punishment* partly to signal his debt for certain observations and partly to differ with Dostoevsky on the limits of individual freedom. All three of these novels figure as major critiques of rationalism and collectivism and as assertions of individual freedom. Both Wright and Ellison apparently learned from Dostoevsky's mature rejection of materialistic social-ism, attacking in similar fashion the cynicism often at the heart of authoritarian, supposedly humanistic organizations and movements. With *Crime and Pun-ishment* Dostoevsky pursues the implications in a full-scale fictional work of the themes that had informed *The House of the Dead*, *Winter Notes on Summer Impressions*, and *Notes from Underground*. He refutes any materialistic justification or logic for murder and argues that natural retribution can claim the murderer and cause him to suffer greatly until he admits his crime and seeks to restore himself to the human community. With Raskolnikov's "infection" with Utilitarian and materialistic ideas, Dostoevsky analyzes what Berdyaev calls "that inward catastrophe from which new souls take their beginning" (*Idea* 202). Dostoevsky poses directly the issue of the worth of human life and concludes that the taking of even the most degraded life, even for seemingly benevolent reasons, may result in terror for the killer and the disintegration of his personality.

Native Son and *The Outsider* both show the considerable influence of *Crime and Punishment*, and Wright's later novel borrows quite liberally from Dostoevsky's for basic themes, situations, characters, and even approximations of dialogue. Just as Dostoevsky recants his former radical affiliations in *The Devils*, with *The Outsider* Wright resolves the ambivalence of *Native Son* on the issue of collectivism. In both of these novels Wright develops Dostoevsky's belief that the human personality will assert its freedom in the most oppressive environment, even to its detriment. Both writers also illustrate the courage needed to accept freedom, as well as the dangers of its unlimited application.

Unlike Dostoevsky, however, Wright presents protagonists whose consciences are basically inactive despite their murders. Dostoevsky uses conscience to show his characters progressing toward a recognition of their evil and a reconnection with humanity; Wright sees the transcendence of conscience as a possible corollary and sign of ultimate freedom. Wright differs from Dostoevsky again in his ambivalent attitude on self-will, implying caution with the destruction of Bigger and Cross, but also stressing self-will as the individual's positive means of creating an identity. These protagonists' failure to discover a social ethic or responsibility to others results in their being stranded in their revolt. The fact that they do not achieve Dostoevsky's second stage of self-abnegation leaves them living out a fascinating "creative nihilism" with which Wright clearly has sympathy but which tends to contribute to what Berdyaev terms "amoral Humanism" (*Idea* 200) and the darkening of personality. Wright's qualified acceptance of this violence and violation of others' rights, in exchange for his characters' heightened freedom and sense of self, diminishes the effectiveness of his rebuttal of determinism and collectivism, which he bases on respect for freedom and dignity.

Wright depicts Bigger and Cross not as heroes outright but as tragic heroes, victims in a sense of their own evolving strength. Both are shown as admirable for their assertion of self-worth and human dignity, and for their choice of a self beyond the constraints of everyday morality. But both unfortunately can discover no limits to their "'right'" to do anything they wish, and their excesses bring about their ruin. Unlike Raskolnikov, Svidrigailov, Stavrogin, Kirilov, Shatov, Ivan Karamazov, and the Invisible Man, as well as Wright's own Fred Daniels of "The Man Who Lived Underground," Bigger and Cross remain, proudly yet tragically, their own gods.

While Dostoevsky in *Crime and Punishment* continues his anti-determinist campaign begun with his other works of the early 1860s, Wright in *Native Son* offers contradictory and confusing attitudes on the crucial matter of Bigger's freedom. Bigger's sudden, and not too convincing development of a metaphysical and an existential sense during his trial results in his acceptance of responsibility for his actions despite the novel's typically naturalistic argument up to that point that the oppressive environment evokes and virtually causes such brutal responses. Wright's lack of resolution toward Marxism, the Communist Party, and naturalism evident in *Native Son* mars its potential ideological and artistic unity. And although it is generally conceded that with *The Outsider* Wright presents a consistent anti-naturalism, the novel does present the world from which Cross escapes as a harsh, smothering environment, a viewpoint typical of naturalistic fiction.

II

In *Crime and Punishment* Dostoevsky reacted to the sudden shift in Russian socialist thought in the early 1860s from idealistic Utopian socialism to nihilism; he strongly opposed the abandonment of the semi-religious glorification of the people for what Frank calls ''the embittered elitism which stressed the right of a superior individual to act independently for the welfare of humanity'' (''World'' 565). Dostoevsky perceived in nihilism the danger of a twisted individualism, the tendency of disgruntled and impatient Utopian socialists to arrogate to themselves the right to follow any course of action as a private enterprise. Nominally they still acted for the common cause of promoting the general betterment of society. But Dostoevsky's point in creating Raskolnikov was to argue that the nihilists' appointing themselves superior or ''exceptional'' individuals and their stepping over ''obstacles'' in the name of logic and reason amounted to nothing more than egoism and self-will, often shrouded in the self-delusion of altruism. *Crime and Punishment* asserts basically that when self-will is mistaken for freedom, murder can be mistaken for benevolence, and that the result for the individual is not liberation but enslavement, not peace but torment. With *The Devils*, published in 1871, Dostoevsky would reflect and oppose the evolution of moral relativism and anarchism which followed from the nihilism of the early and mid-1860s. The declension from Raskolnikov to Peter Verkhovensky and Stavrogin of *The Devils* traces the development of horrid, motiveless evil partly as a reaction against the well-intentioned but impotent idealism of the generation of the forties. But while dealing in *Crime and Punishment* with nihilism and the middle stage of the continuum from idealistic superfluousness to amoral relativism, Dostoevsky depicts the contradiction of what Wright calls straightforwardly in *The Outsider* the dilemma of the ''ethical criminal,'' of benevolence and idealism still residing in an individual like Raskolnikov, who claims the right even to murder to realize his identity and to achieve his goals as a "superior" individual.

Dostoevsky represents the public quarrel between 1863 and 1865 between the old Utopian socialists and the new nihilists by the markedly different aims and characters of Lebezyatnikov and Raskolnikov. Frank describes the contrast between

> the comic and harmless Utopian socialist in the novel, Lebezyat-
> nikov, and Raskolnikov himself, who is no longer a Utopian
> socialist but a true Nihilist. The Utopian socialist is in favor of
> peaceful propaganda, conversion to the cause by reason and
> persuasion, and he believes that the salvation of humanity hinges
> on communal living arrangements. . . . Raskolnikov looks on all
> this as ineffectual nonsense; he feels that time is running out . . .
> that the superior individual has the right and the obligation to
> strike a decisive blow by himself. ("World" 565)

The exchanges between Lebezyatnikov and Luzhin represent exaggerations of English Utilitarianism and positivist views. Thus, through caricature Dostoevsky ridicules the early phase of Russian materialism as incorporating a mixture of intellectually bankrupt ideas, kindness of heart, and stupidity. But quite unlike the Iago-like malignity of Peter Verkhovensky or the athletic willfulness and moral relativism of Stavrogin, Lebezyatnikov's misdirection is innocent of any evil intentions. Lebezyatnikov parrots the proper liberal cliches, imbibed from Chernyshevsky's *What Is to Be Done?* such as the need for attention to the "woman's question" and for experimental communal living based on rational principles which supposedly will organize an environment to eliminate evil altogether. Though a comically stupid fellow, and occasionally hypocritical (as demonstrated in the beating of Mrs. Marmeladov, a downtrodden woman), Lebezyatnikov at least maintains something of a good heart and some degree of honesty, as seen when he tells the truth about Luzhin's plot to disgrace Sonya. Luzhin, a slave of bourgeois respectability, feigns interest in the progressive materialistic ideas in the air in Petersburg mainly out of an attachment to fashion. His attempt to ruin Sonya represents the most conventionally villain-like or blackguardly deed of the novel, but of course it pales alongside Raskolnikov's murders.

Raskolnikov has not accepted the new Utilitarian and positivistic ideas wholesale, but he does subscribe to the basic rationalism and materialism which underlie them. Planning the murder, as Frank says, "on the basis of a Utilitarian calculus," Raskolnikov believes "that his reason can overcome the most fundamental and deeply rooted human feelings" ("World" 564). *Crime and Punishment* features the typical Dostoevskian struggle of a young member of the intelligentsia "torn . . . between the irrational (which is always moral) and the amorality of reason" ("World" 567). Dostoevsky uses the character and fate of Raskolnikov as an attack on all systems or movements based on rationalism, materialism, and/or the will to power, and as a defense of the inviolable value of all human life and of the definition of man as a spiritual being. Raskolnikov is Dostoevsky's major example of the failure of humanism, of ethics without morality; Raskolnikov's attempt to justify murder based on logic and the "simple arithmetic" of being able to help more people in the future founders on the simple but overwhelming presence and activity of his conscience.

One of the most basic theses of the novel finds explicit expression in the *Notebooks*:

> The truth of God and the law of nature take their own and he finally feels forced to give himself up, in order to be once again part of human kind, even if it means perishing in prison. The feeling of isolation and separation from humanity which he felt immediately after committing the crime wears him down. . . . Legal punishment for a crime frightens a criminal much less than we think because the criminal himself morally demands it. (172)

Vyacheslav Ivanov points out that Dostoevsky objected to the deterministic theories about crime, which were gaining in popularity in the 1860s and which tend to negate the idea of individual responsibility: "For they take from man his freedom and nobility, his divine dignity. No, the criminal must, and wants to, accept retribution for the act that expresses the metaphysical self-determination of his free will" (*Freedom* 82). Indeed, if one attempts to deny the criminal's free will, the criminal act loses both something of its horror as well as its potential regenerative side-effect through the operations of conscience. Alexander Bem suggests that a crime can become a catastrophic event only if guilt is present (626). Wright attempts to exorcise or deny guilt (as a sense of having done "wrong") in his rebel-criminals, adding to our shock and horror and therefore to the novels' power and effect. But the absence of such an inner conflict denies a further psychological dimension to these characters and lessens our sympathy for them. Consequently, neither of Wright's novels considered here attains a level of catastrophe or tragedy comparable to *Crime and Punishment*.

Raskolnikov's experiment in applied materialism consists of his attempt to prove that conscience and the categories of right and wrong simply do not exist for (and therefore have no sway over) the superior individual. He thinks that he can avoid the typical criminal's breakdown of concentration or "collapse of will-power and reason" (60) which thwarts his escape or freedom from suspicion. Raskolnikov decides that he will not be subject to the weakness or illness which often attends the commission of a major crime. In essence, he tries to deny the spiritual reality of guilt: "He decided that he personally would not be subject to any such morbid subversion, that his judgment and will would remain steadfast throughout the fulfillment of his plans, for the simple reason that what he contemplated was 'no crime'" (61). In response to Porfiry's question about the plight of the "exceptional" man who finds that he *has* a conscience, Raskolnikov sums up his own situation as it will shortly develop: "Any man who has one must suffer if he is conscious of error. That is his punishment--in addition to hard labor" (224). Because of his lingering feelings of compassion and because of his avowed motive of helping others with the fruits of his murder, he is abhorred at moments by the depravity of pure logic; Dostoevsky shows him mocking the coldness of reason as it computes the "necessity" of using young girls such as Sonya as prostitutes: "Such and such a percentage they say, must go every year. . . . A percentage! They have some capital words: they are so soothing and scientific'' (43). But his commitment to rationalism, though a rationalization for testing his status as an exceptional man for whom everything is permitted, demands that he recoil from his first generous and human impulses in many situations. Raskolnikov seeks a consistency of motive and thought along rationalistic and Utilitarian lines which he never achieves, for he is never able to kill off his deeply rooted sense of concern for others. Even though he mocks himself for leaving the Marmeladovs money, for helping the young girl pursued by the stranger on the street, and for several similar actions after the murders, that compassionate part of his character in fact ironically grows as he comes to learn that benevolence and compassion had nothing to do with the murders. At his first meeting with Luzhin, he suggests with disdain and self-righteousness that the logical extension of the doctrine of self-interest is the license to cut people's throats. The pain of the realization that he killed not for anyone else but for himself-- in spite of his own belief in self-advantage--results in the humiliating knowledge of his weakness and destroys his glorified self-image as an exceptional individual.

In the *Notebooks for Crime and Punishment* Dostoevsky refers implicitly to the novel's basic thesis that conscience and guilt are inescapable phenomenological realities: "Is there a law of nature that we don't know and which cries out in us?" (66). Aesthetic repulsion for the murder strikes Raskolnikov even before the event, and what Ivanov refers to as "the revelation of mystic guilt" (*Freedom* 78) begins immediately after. With the crime comes precisely that "disease" or disordering of the mind that Raskolnikov was so certain he would surmount--and, therefore, also the pained though initially repressed consciousness that he has failed to prove himself a Napoleon for whom such acts are supposedly allowable. As Bem suggests, "His intellect feels no repentance until the very end. . . . Yet his whole being, his moral structure, is shaken by the moral aspect of the murder'' (626). Raskolnikov momentarily decides to confess quite early in his struggle, after the taunting interview with Zamyetov, both from shame that he has not proven to be an exceptional man and from an unconscious sense that he may not be able to bear the isolation and guilt (which on the conscious level he denies).

The operation of unconscious guilt on the spirit of Raskolnikov enables him to recover his relationship with humanity and eventually to surrender his belief in logic and reason. He feels a strong upsurge of life within him as, upon the death of Marmeladov he takes on responsibilities for the care of the family. Both his often-repeated phrase ''I will pay!'' (150) regarding the medical and funeral expenses, and his startled admission that he is indeed covered in the blood of the dead Marmeladov, suggest his re-entry into human relationships and foreshadow his acceptance of responsibility for the murders. At times he mocks Sonya because she is simple and because she represents, in Bem's words, ''the pressure of the law of nature crying out within him'' (627). But his decision to trust her with his secret marks his turning point toward confession and reparation. The strongest suggestion of Raskolnikov's drift from the rationalism which has figured prominently in his justification of killing occurs in a conversation with Lebezyatnikov just before the haze of indecision settles on him at the opening of Part Six: Raskolnikov ignores Lebezyatnikov completely as the latter explains the wonders of experiments to cure the insane by the use of logical persuasion. A moment later Raskolnikov reflects that ''perhaps it really would be better to go to Siberia'' (359). Dostoevsky suggests Raskolnikov's transition from unconscious to dimly conscious feelings of conscience early in Part Six by actually using the word ''conscience'': ''He suddenly became uneasy again, as though the pangs of conscience had begun to torment him; 'Here I sit listening to songs, but surely that is not what I ought to be doing,' he thought'' (372).

The final and crucial stage of Raskolnikov's surrender of rationalism and pride takes place in the much-debated Epilogue and coincides with his implicit final realization of the moral evil of the murders. During his illness through

Lent and Easter, and just preceding his conversion, he dreams of a form of rationalism which literally infects people worldwide and brings about intellectual arrogance, solipsism, and ultimately complete social chaos and decay. Thus Raskolnikov sees imaginatively the destructive effects of his rationalistic theory applied universally. Although the Epilogue is often criticized with some reason as psychologically and artistically unconvincing, Dostoevsky wisely refrains from attempting to present in just a few pages a Raskolnikov utterly transformed from a still defiant inmate who sees the murders as no crime, to a fully reborn individual. Yet Dostoevsky carefully delineates the outlines of the significant changes in his protagonist; most importantly, Raskolnikov has learned that there *is* a law of psychological and moral retribution for "mistakes" or evil. At his moment of recognition or conversion, prepared for by Dostoevsky's use of patterns of traditional Christian imagery (Gibian 519-36), Raskolnikov's education in the natural law is completed with his surrender of egoistic pride and an openness to a "new future, a perfect resurrection into a new life" (463). He passes his first evening of new life delivered from the enslavement of rationalism, no longer reasoning, but feeling, living: "But this evening he could not think long or coherently of anything or concentrate his attention on any idea, and indeed he was not consciously reasoning at all; he could only feel. Life had taken the place of logic and something quite different must be worked out in his mind" (464).

Dostoevsky rejects the modern, rationalistic, deterministic view that crime is essentially a function of a poor environment; he will surrender neither man's freedom nor his responsibility. Although in places the narrator seems to give credence to the idea of the operation of chance or fate in the commission of the murders, Dostoevsky ironically and subtly suggests that this is how Raskolnikov seeks to deny his responsibility and to be comforted by his self-deceit. Raskolnikov minimizes the role of his freedom in the stages leading up to the murders, and blames fate, special circumstances and influences, the devil--anyone but himself--for his gravitation toward the crime. The deterministic speculations belong to the mind of Raskolnikov, as he reflects, for example, that "it was almost as if fate had laid an ambush for him" (52) or "as if special coincidences and influences were at work" (54). The most explicit statement in the novel of Dostoevsky's rejection of determinism occurs in Razumikhin's heated indictment of Utopian socialism for explaining "everything by the 'deleterious influence of the environment'--and that's all! Their favorite cliche" (216). In a brief restatement of the thesis of *Notes from Underground*, Razumikhin, who stands for moderation and good sense, attacks the materialists' attempt to ignore nature: "That is why they do not like the living process of life: they have no use for the living soul. The living soul demands life, the living soul will not submit to mechanism" (217).

Throughout the novel Dostoevsky demonstrates, also in the manner of *Notes from Underground*, the peculiar risk and intoxication one experiences in defying logic, sticking out one's tongue at rationalism, and asserting his freedom in even the most disadvantageous circumstances. Raskolnikov's "almost unendurable pleasure" (141) in taunting Zamyetov with the truth about the murders, together with his going to the flat afterwards to look for the blood and his initial decision to tell the police everything, figure as some of the more memorable instances of the indomitable resurgence of freedom even in the psyche consciously committed to exclusively rational action. To underscore this major theme, Dostoevsky transposes the story from *The House of the Dead* of the submissive convict who "for a whole year lay on the stove at night reading his bible, and read and read until he was in such a state that suddenly, without rhyme or reason, he grabbed a brick and threw it at the governor, without the slightest provocation" (*Crime* 384). Porfiry explains to Raskolnikov the paradox of freedom, that while it fills one with life and power, it also can become an insupportable burden, especially to the person who has fractured the moral order: "The point is that he won't run away because he has nowhere to run to, but that psychologically he won't escape! . . . Freedom will no longer be a boon to him; he will begin to brood, he will get himself into a muddle, entangle his own feet in a net, and worry himself to death!'' (287).

Although Dostoevsky uses Raskolnikov to represent the evolution of radical thought in Russia in the early 1860s from Utopian socialism to nihilism, he emphasizes these ideologies' shared philosophical materialism and the tendency of both toward despotism--tendencies criticized by Wright and Ellison as well. While Raskolnikov generally has sympathy for the socialists, he distinguishes their common goals from his consciously isolated, selfish ones:

> Why was that foolish fellow Razumikhin railing at the Socialists just now? They are industrious and businesslike people; they work for the "common weal."... No, I have only one life given to me, and it will never come again; I do not want to wait for the "common weal." I want to have my own life, or else it is better not to live at all. (233)

But in a letter Dostoevsky underlined the socialists' and nihilists' essentially similar world-view and their shared idealistic devotion to truth:

> All nihilists are socialists. Socialism (particularly in its Russian form) demands especially the severing of all connections. They are completely certain that on the *tabula rasa* they will immediately build a paradise. . . . But all these high school students, schoolboys of whom I have seen so many converted to nihilism so purely, so selflessly in the name of honor, truth, and true welfare . . . the poor little people are convinced that nihilism gives them that full manifestation of their civic and social reality and freedom. ("Letters," *Crime* 479)

While Dostoevsky admires the strong convictions of the socialists, he finds their rage for freedom materialistic and therefore self-defeating: "The main idea of socialism is mechanism. There man is made man by mechanics. Rules for everything. Man himself is removed. . . . Socialism is the despair ever to put man in order. They build despotism and say it is freedom ("Notebooks," *Crime* 475).

Svidrigailov figures as another individual who attempts to disprove the existence of conscience and the natural moral law; but despite his dedication to a life of willful aesthetics and conscious moral relativism, he too is pursued by guilt until it effects a transformation of his being which foreshadows that of Raskolnikov. Much like Stavrogin of *The Devils*, Svidrigailov lives in conscious despair which has culminated in an act (or acts, in Svidrigailov's case) of virtual murder and which he masks by a hedonistic pursuit of pleasure and flight from boredom. Unlike Raskolnikov, Svidrigailov has neither any idealism nor any link to an ideology such as socialism or nihilism. Commonly analyzed as Raskolnikov's double, Svidrigailov functions as a chilling and unlikely pioneer in the realm of spirit, experiencing strangely mundane but undeniably otherworldly visitations by the ghosts of his wife, a servant, and a young girl he has violated, for all of whose deaths he is responsible. Yet despite both his direct, phenomenological awareness of the spiritual and his lecture to Raskolnikov on apparitions as "fragments of other worlds" (244), he continues his losing fight against boredom and despair only by miring himself further in sensations. Dostoevsky illustrates the danger and the hope for Raskolnikov as Svidrigailov gravitates toward his suicide; for as Raskolnikov gradually becomes conscious of the despair of his own refusal to confess, he sees that Svidrigailov's parallel case clarifies his only other option.

Svidrigailov's surprising and evidently genuine love for Dunya, transformed from lust by his deepening (but still resisted) sense of spirituality and of unconscious remorse, delivers him temporarily from complete despair, for at the moment when he is about to violate her, he chooses to let her go. This implicit birth of real sensitivity and of moral choice in Svidrigailov, which augurs well for Raskolnikov, is further suggested by the former's benevolent arrangements for his fiancee and by his wish to do good for Dunya: "I earnestly desire--not to buy myself off, not to pay for the unpleasantness, but purely and simply to do something for her good" (247). Svidrigailov commits suicide as a reluctant judgment against his now-abandoned relativism and also as a condemnation of his past, which has rendered Dunya unattainable. He kills himself not from boredom, which had been his motivation in contemplating the act, but from despair of ever being happy and of being able to live with his now oppressive guilt. His brilliantly rendered last night is filled with visions of the violated young girl who took her own life. Svidrigailov's "nightmares all night long" (431) prevent his suicide until dawn, suggesting that there is still time for Raskolnikov and that his active conscience offers his best hope for survival. The suicide of Svidrigailov may be said to take on a sacrificial aspect because he has done much good for the Marmeladovs (especially Sonya), for his fiancee (by not marrying her, and by providing for her), and for Raskolnikov, by not informing the police. Svidrigailov's suicide is sacrificial also because he takes on himself, so to speak, the darker of the two alternatives available to Raskolnikov and thus diverts him from a similar fate. Raskolnikov's disappearance and wandering in the rain throughout Svidrigailov's last night suggest his proximity also to a decision of suicide. Raskolnikov's decision to confess, arrived at without conscious knowledge of Svidrigailov's fate, still proceeds largely from a certainty that Svidrigailov would take his own life. Thus Dostoevsky demonstrates the closely intertwined failures of both characters' projects in materialism and their attempted denials of the natural law. Though both Raskolnikov and Svidrigailov at first proclaim themselves ultimately free, both become bound by their different varieties of self-will; both, however, come to realize some degree of freedom in the end through measures of reparation and social connection.

III

Nikolai Berdyaev offers some of the most precise and insightful critical analysis of Raskolnikov, and his comments can be applied to Bigger Thomas and Cross Damon to illustrate Wright's inversion of Dostoevsky's thesis. Berdyaev summarizes the dilemma of the free man evident in *Crime and Punishment*, *Native Son*, and *The Outsider*: "Are there norms and limits in my nature, or may I venture to do anything?" ("Dostoevsky" 574). He holds with Dostoevsky that the individual loses his freedom when he defies all limitations:

> When freedom has degenerated into self-will it recognizes nothing as sacred or forbidden. . . . Raskolnikov does not give the impression of a free man at all but of a maniac possessed by vicious delusions; there is no sign of that moral independence that goes with self-purification and self-liberation. . . . After his crime . . . he lost his freedom. . . . He had learned that it is easy to kill a man but that spiritual and not physical energy is expended in the doing of it. ("Dostoevsky" 574-75)

Wright does admit, especially with Cross, the possible enslavement and dehumanization of the individual by his own affirmation. But he does not reject altogether the man who has gone beyond the sacred and the forbidden. Berdyaev agrees with Dostoevsky that such individualism only degrades the person:

> The case of Raskolnikov illustrates the crisis of Humanism, what its morality leads to, the suicide of man by his self-affirmation. . . . There is no humanitarianism left in Raskolnikov, who is cruel and without pity for his neighbor. . . . Thus the god-man kills true manhood, as can be seen in the example of Nietzsche. The Marxist ideal of an inhuman collectivism is equally deadly for mankind. ("Dostoevsky" 576)

Berdyaev finds in all Dostoevsky's novels man going through "this spiritual process, through freedom and evil to redemption" ("Dostoevsky" 574). The notion of redemption is foreign to most of Wright's work, where man is a permanently superfluous being in a hostile universe and God has returned to the level of myth. Wright's protagonists Bigger and Cross literally "see no evil" in their actions, as they are suspended in their self-destructive defiance.

Native Son's primary focus of social protest in the name of collective organization is obscured and reversed to some degree by its late shift toward an ostensible defense of individual dignity, as Wright attempts to make Bigger into an existential hero with an intense and explicit consciousness of his freedom. With this direction Wright at least begins to move away from collectivism and toward a more conscious and more consistent treatment of the problem of the individual, to be found in *The Outsider*. But his major novels do not convince the reader completely that the black man, or any man, can be either so oppressed or so "free" as to leave all effects of conscience behind--whether as a sensitivity he cannot afford because of injustice against him (as in *Native Son*), or as unnecessary baggage from an earlier stage of man's moral evolution (as in *The Outsider*). Wright's central assertion of human dignity and freedom is compromised somewhat by his representation of two partly heroic figures who are exempt from remorse at the violation of other individuals' dignity and freedom. Neither Bigger nor Cross experiences conscious revulsion or guilt at the horror of his deeds. Cross especially seems to succeed in exactly the materialistic project which Raskolnikov sets for himself, namely to prove that for the superior person there is no right or wrong, and therefore no guilt. Even Bigger avoids the "disease" (as Raskolnikov calls it) of weakness and moral feeling as Wright offers his first, tentative exploration of the limits of freedom and self-will. Wright develops his flawed "superman" with the awkwardly existential Bigger partly as a result of his dissatisfaction with materialistic collectivism and naturalism. *Native Son* and *The Outsider* reflect the evolution of Wright's thought toward a materialistic individualism, according to which even persons who commit the most cold-blooded murders remain innocent to a considerable degree. This innocence is asserted not because of their author's waning belief in deterministic naturalism, which tends to excuse individual culpability because of the malforming influences of environment, but because of his incipient existentialism and the feeling that the acceptance of freedom places one beyond conventional morality's ability to judge behavior.

A major thesis of *Crime and Punishment* holds that the commission of a crime or an evil act *can* result paradoxically in a positive development of the personality that might have been impossible otherwise. Dostoevsky refers to this idea in a letter concerning the novel: "'From this crime itself begins his moral development, the possibility of such questions as earlier were impossible" ("Notebooks" 473). Wright works this theme with Bigger and Cross, suggesting that each man's life of consciousness and freedom begins only with the commission of a murder. Bigger's acceptance of a minimal level of responsibility for the unintentional killing of Mary Dalton does indeed signal the beginning of his consciousness as a free moral agent. But Cross Damon's new consciousness begins with the passive, external event of the train wreck and his subsequent prospect of creating a completely new life for himself; his killings are virtually gratuitous acts so far as the development of his new personality is concerned, and he never accepts any responsibility for them, denying their significance and his guilt up to his death. Wright appropriates Dostoevsky's thesis only in a narrow sense, ignoring its dialectical application: that the crime or immoral act proves ultimately liberating only if the individual ultimately recognizes the evil, confesses and/or repents, and finds meaning in a renewed relationship to humanity. Dostoevsky claims that evil can lead dialectically to the birth of a new and better person, but that if that evil is not apprehended as such, the individual heads rapidly toward not self-realization but self-destruction. In another important reference to *Crime and Punishment*, Dostoevsky adds that "out of despair there comes a new perspective" ("Notebooks" 472), implying a rebirth such as he suggests in the Epilogue. Both Bigger and Cross can be said to gain something of a new perspective from their nihilistic actions, but according to Dostoevsky's view their despair only deepens and becomes what Kierkegaard calls the "sickness unto death." Their symbolic protest against the environmental persecution of the individual (Bigger) or his cosmic persecution (Cross) is weakened by their offenses against human dignity. The idea of the interrelation of the human community and the corporate experience of salvation was deeply ingrained in nineteenth-century Russian thought, as exemplified by Solovyov's statement that "it is only together with all other human beings that the individual can really be saved" (96). Wright approaches this attitude in "The Man Who Lived Underground" and to a lesser degree in *The Outsider*, but in *Native Son* he minimizes the individual's responsibility to others and rejects the notion of salvation itself.

In spite of Wright's attempts in *Native Son* to convince his readers and, one senses, himself, that he still believes in naturalism and collectivism, his position is often confused and contradictory, divided by his incipient interest in representing a free individual whose actions are not controlled by social or environmental forces. Margolies summarizes the root contradiction of the novel: "Since moral responsibility involves choice, how can Wright's deterministic Marxism be reconciled with the freedom of action that choice implies? The contradiction is never resolved, and for this reason the novel fails to fulfill itself" (107). Indeed, in many places in the novel Wright does not seem to know whether he wants to show Bigger as fated or free. In "How Bigger Was Born," his introduction to the novel, he evidently attempts to bolster his deterministic position or to head off possible criticism of its inconsistencies. His clarification stresses the power of environment but ignores the novel's late, opposing existentialist theme of freedom and partial responsibility:

> I don't mean to say that I think that environment *makes* consciousness (I suppose God makes that, if there is a God), but I do say that I felt and still feel that the environment supplies the instrumentalities through which the organism expresses itself, and if that environment is warped or tranquil, the mode and manner of behavior will be affected toward deadlocking tensions of orderly fulfillment and satisfaction. (xvi)

In order to reinforce his naturalistic roots, Wright echoes Zola's thesis of the scientific nature of his work:

> Why should I not, like a scientist in a laboratory, use my imagination and invent test-tube situations, place Bigger in them, and, following the guidance of my own hopes and fears, what I had learned and remembered, work out in fictional form an emotional statement and resolution of this problem? (xxi)

The patently naturalistic tone dominates the first two-thirds of *Native Son*, which Fabre calls "an act of defiance, an ideological bomb with which Wright frankly proclaimed his fear, his sense of deprivation and hatred" (*Quest* 37). Herbert Hill observes that "the framework of *Native Son* is to be found in the implicit assumption that the social order is directly responsible for the degradation of the Negro, that American society produces conditions that distort and destroy individual human beings who are part of an oppressed group" (5).

Strong naturalistic overtones begin early in Book One of *Native Son* with Bigger's sense of entrapment and fate: "I feel like something awful's going to happen to me. . . . It's like I was going to do something I can't help" (24). His choosing the seemingly safe course of refusing to rob the white store results in his getting the job at the Daltons', but this choice also ironically and somewhat perversely sets in motion the events leading to his destruction; his fate pursues him despite his efforts to avoid trouble. As an unfree pawn of destiny, Bigger feels no responsibility either toward himself or to others. In the scene where the newsmen in the Dalton basement discover the bones in the furnace, Wright suggests Bigger's helplessness: "He felt that he had let things slip through his hands to such an extent that he could not get at them again" (204). Bigger's acceptance of some general responsibility for Mary's death--which clearly is no murder, but essentially a brutish accident--allows Bigger to experience freedom as a moral agent for the first time in his life; but Wright continues to inject straightforward naturalistic material into his narrative even after Bigger's much more freely realized second killing, the brutal murder of Bessie Mears. Bigger reflects after Mary's death that "all his life he had been knowing that sooner or later something like this would come to him" (207). In describing Bigger's thoughts prior to the killing of Bessie, Wright minimizes and virtually negates the element of Bigger's responsibility and freedom, and thus he contradicts his own tentative existentialist thesis: "He thought of it calmly, as if the decision were being handed down to him by some logic not his own, over which he had no control, but which he had to obey" (215). After Bessie's murder Wright echoes the argument of environment, which serves as the focal point of his social protest in the novel, at the expense of his nascent emphasis on individual choice:

> He had been so conditioned in a cramped environment that hard words or kicks alone knocked him upright and made him capable of action--action that was futile because the world was too much for him.... He had been caught up in a whirl of thought and feeling which had swept him onward. (226)

Wright's somewhat halting and, some critics suggest, half-baked existentialism in *Native Son* contends with his naturalism; and his failure to resolve this contradiction seriously weakens the still considerable power of this novel. In the first stages of Bigger's flight after Mary's death, he "felt that he had his destiny in his grasp. He was more alive than he could ever remember having been.... The feeling of being always enclosed in the stifling embrace of an invisible force had gone from him" (142). Just before Bessie's murder, Wright moves swiftly from a determinist-tinged justification for or explanation of it (quoted above), to a quite contrary statement of Bigger's new freedom, stressing his choice and control over his life: "The moment he stepped out of that door he would have his life in his hands. Whatever happened now depended upon him; and when he felt it that way some of his fear left; it was simple again" (216). Wright's often-quoted comment on Bigger's new freedom constitutes a rather explicit intrusion into the narrative, but at least he clarifies the rising anti-determinist strain: "*He* had done this. *He* had brought this about. ... Never had his will been so free as in this night and day of fear and murder and flight" (225). By his "supreme act of will" he accepts "responsibility for that murder because it had made him feel free for the first time in his life" (255). These manifestly existentialist pronouncements, offered too explicitly by Wright to be subtle or completely convincing, continue to the end of the novel; for example, as Bigger rejects hope and religious faith from his jail cell, Wright notes that "whatever he thought or did from now on would have to come from him and him alone" (315).

In spite of *Native Son*'s admixture of existentialist themes, Ellison came to criticize what he saw as its extreme emphasis on environment and the passivity and helplessness of the individual. In "Richard Wright's Blues," an early essay on the autobiography *Black Boy*, Ellison defended Wright's naturalism, maintaining that "in the South the sensibilities of both blacks and whites are inhibited in the rigidly defined environment" (205). In another essay written eighteen years later, however, he criticized *Black Boy* for its harsh indictment of black life and implied that the work had been fashioned to conform to Marxist ideology (O'Meally 45). Similarly, Ellison's first comments on *Native Son*, in "Richard Wright and Negro Fiction," were laudatory but general; some twenty years later, he rejected Bigger as little more than a sociological and ideological construct whose deterministic conception offended Ellison's sense of human possibility and freedom:

> Bigger Thomas was presented as a near-subhuman indictment of white oppression. He was designed to shock whites out of their apathy and end the circumstances out of which Wright insisted Bigger emerged. Here environment is all--and interestingly enough, environment conceived solely in terms of the physical, the non-conscious. (*Shadow* 114)

Wright's evident vacillation between naturalism and existentialism is paralleled by his ambivalence toward collectivism and the Communist Party.

With *Native Son* his intended defense of individual dignity emerges with more force and clarity than in *Uncle Tom's Children*, and his qualified personalism begins to supersede the banner of collectivism. He begins to suspect quite publicly that while collectivism as represented by the Communist Party may seek to further the cause of individual political liberty, it fails to apprehend the deeper reality and the more autonomous value of human dignity and the preservation of the human personality. For Wright, then, although social protest guided the inception and much of the incarnation of *Native Son*, it became overshadowed by the phenomenon of individual revolt as a universal aspect of humanity.

One detects Wright's weakening commitment to the Party first in his compensatory, propagandistic, and artistically wooden defense of it. He strains to make Bigger symbolic of oppressed people presumably because of his guilty consciousness on some level that he would soon abandon communist ideology and propaganda. In the novel's introduction, Wright confides that he conceived of Bigger ideologically, "as a meaningful and prophetic symbol.... My contact with the labor movement and its ideology made me see Bigger clearly, and feel what he meant" (xiv). Baldwin objects to the novel's limiting itself to "mere" protest, which can too often be ''an accepted and comforting aspect of the American scene. . . . Below the surface of this novel there lies a continuation, a complement of that monstrous legend it was written to destroy'' (*Notes* 22). Margolies finds it "transparently propagandistic" because

> with the exception of Bigger, none of the characters is portrayed
> in any depth--and most of them are depicted as representative
> "types" of the social class to which they belong. . . . Wright
> succumbs to the occupational disease of proletarian authors by
> hammering home sociological points in didactic expository prose
> when they could just as clearly be understood in terms of the
> organic development of the novel. (105)

Wright offers Jan Erlone quite didactically as Bigger's potential savior, but the shallowness of Jan's depiction and his supposedly deep understanding of the suffering of blacks such as Bigger undermines the communist solution which Wright proposes for amending the privations of black life in America. Wright, commenting that "the word had become flesh" (268) with Jan's openness to Bigger after the latter's attempt to discredit the Party, tries to rescue Jan from his early characterization as a well-intentioned but experientially insincere proponent of black rights; but the transformation fails, and Wright strays into incredibility. Brignano links Wright's propagandistic use of Jan with his failure to represent convincingly his sympathetic white characters:

> With the appearance of Jan Erlone ... the novel becomes blatantly propagandistic.... The fact that throughout the novel Jan remains an undeveloped, insufficiently motivated figure may indicate either that Wright could not fully believe the probability that racially unprejudiced whites do exist, or that he could not deal convincingly with white or white-Communist psychology. (79)

Other heavy-handed devices used by Wright to secure sympathy for the Party include his characterization of the prosecuting attorney as one-dimensionally racist and monstrous, and his making preachy, liberal points through the defense lawyer Max (e.g., "This boy comes from an oppressed people. Even if he's done wrong, we must take that into consideration." 273).

A second and more direct indication of Wright's drifting from wholehearted support of the Party lies in his frank criticism of the shallow interior commitment of many communists and liberals. Kinnamon's claim that Wright maintains a "thoroughly Communist point of view in *Native Son*" (125) is refuted by even a slight acquaintance with the novel. Wright himself, sensing that the Party would not approve unreservedly a protagonist who balks at communist salvation and who mouths a philosophy of freedom and individual action, admits in his introduction some anxiety over Party reaction but stands firm on his primary and deepening commitment to individual rights and freedom, both of protagonists and authors:

> What would my own white and black comrades in the Communist

> Party say. . . . Though my heart is with the collectivist ideal, I
> solved this problem by assuring myself that honest politics and
> honest feeling in imaginative representation ought to be able to
> meet on common healthy ground without fear, suspicion, and
> quarreling. . . . I felt that a right more immediately deeper than that
> of politics or race was at stake; that is, a *human* right, the right of
> a man to think and feel honestly. (xxii)

Bigger has a few moments of sympathy for Jan near the novel's end, but for the most part his initial, instinctive mistrust and rejection of liberals and communists is sustained by his further knowledge of them.

In the novel's latter stages, as Wright contradictorily steps up both his propagandistic speechifying in favor of the Party and Bigger's existentialism, Bigger abandons Jan's advice and confesses. Wright does point out that there is an element of humanity and dignity in the treatment Bigger receives from Mary and Jan (66). But Wright reserves a good share of his indignation for such "sensitive," liberal whites as Mary and Jan because they tantalize Bigger with treatment resembling but ultimately parodistic of dignity. Their treatment of Bigger purports to recognize personality but only teases and crushes it with their insensitivity and fundamental inhumanity. Wright criticizes liberals such as the Daltons, people with obviously shallow knowledge of blacks; he finds at least as culpable, however, those like Mary and Jan, whose unintentional but quite real insincerity proves so dangerous to Bigger. Indeed, their failure to understand the suffering they inflict on him drives Bigger to the first killing as much as his environment does. Thus, Bigger's letter to the Daltons assigning blame to the Party may be taken as a symbolic expression of Wright's partly repressed but emerging attitude.

Most of Wright's early fiction up to *Native Son* deals in graphic (and, some say, sensationalized) violence committed by both whites and blacks. The violence performed by blacks almost always figures as an excusable, or at least understandable response of self-defense to a direct threat on a person's life. With *Native Son* and *The Outsider*, however, Wright leaves behind the situation of direct self-defense, and the killing in these later works becomes to some extent gratuitous. In *Native Son* he shows that Bigger kills in response to a hostile and threatening environment, but nowhere do we see someone on the brink of murdering Bigger. *The Outsider* abandons for the most part the previous sociological and naturalistic framework, and the multiple cold-blooded murders of Cross Damon become even more problematical.

In the introduction to *Native Son* Wright makes explicit his intention that Bigger's actions be unsympathetic and indefensible. In analyzing *Uncle Tom's Children* Wright comments:

> I found that I had written a book which even bankers' daughters could read and weep over and feel good about. I swore to myself that if I ever wrote another book, no one would weep over it; that it would have to be so hard and deep that they would have to face it without the consolation of tears. (xxvii)

But there are, to say the least, extenuating circumstances surrounding Bigger's first killing which mitigate his personal responsibility. First, as mentioned earlier, his unwilling association with Jan and Mary contributes largely to Mary's death. Second and more important, her killing in no sense qualifies as an intentional or premeditated murder: as Wright takes special pains to emphasize, Bigger's stifling Mary with a pillow may be a brutal, stupid act; but it involves neither premeditation nor intent, nor even knowledge of what was actually taking place. The hate and humiliation which Jan and Mary have stirred up in Bigger find expression in a forceful physical act, but clearly he never intends harm to her. Wright, contrary to his expressed intention of avoiding pity and tears, secures much sympathy for Bigger by depicting him not as a monster but as a *victim* of circumstance, accident, and a hostile environment.

Later in the novel Wright confuses the moral (and legal) issue of the first killing by referring to it unqualifiedly as a murder while he strains to make a point critical of Christianity: "He had killed himself the preacher's haunting

picture of life even before he had killed Mary; that had been his first murder"
(264). Wright allows his spokesman in Bigger's defense, the lawyer Mr. Max,
to further confound the central moral issue of intention and guilt by focusing
on the mere sociological and deterministic interpretation of the incident: "Let
us not concern ourselves with that part of Bigger Thomas's confession that says
he murdered accidentally, that he did not rape the girl. It really does not matter.
What does matter is that he was guilty *before* he killed!" (369). Max, in arguing
that not even the premeditated murder of Bessie should be called murder,
sounds like an unintentional parody of the slick but insincere defense attorney
in *The Brothers Karamazov*, who cynically assumes his client's guilt and
argues that Dmitry killed his father in cold blood but still should not be judged
a murderer. Max argues:

> But did Bigger Thomas really murder? . . . Looked at from the
> outside, maybe it was murder; yes. But to him it was not murder.
> . . . The truth is, this boy did *not* kill! Oh yes; Mary Dalton is dead.
> Bigger Thomas smothered her to death. Bessie Mears is dead.
> Bigger Thomas battered her with a brick in an abandoned building.
> But did he murder? . . . He was *living*, only as he knew how, and
> as we have forced him to live. The actions that resulted in the death
> of those two women were as instinctive and inevitable as breathing
> or blinking one's eyes. It was an act of *creation*! (366)

Thus Wright questionably associates the tragic and destructive act with
creativity and liberation.

Wright's handling of Bigger's second killing, the only real murder, the
cold-blooded bludgeoning of Bessie, demonstrates Wright's departure from
Dostoevsky's position in *Crime and Punishment*. Wright attempts to strip this
murder, described in typically graphic detail, of its simple, concrete meaning
for the murderer and the murdered, and offers instead only ideological,
sociological, and philosophical abstractions for his various didactic purposes.
First, he confuses the issue of the murder by implying through the narrator that
Bigger has a legitimate motive of self-protection, that Bigger's survival

demands the removal of Bessie: "What could he do with her? . . . Coldly, he knew that he had to take her with him, and then at some future time settle things with her, settle them in a way that would not leave him in any danger" (215). Thus Wright offers a virtual parody of his earlier theme of legitimate self-defense, exhibited throughout *Uncle Tom's Children*. Second, Wright's determinist thesis also overshadows the fact of Bessie's murder. As discussed earlier, Wright at times squarely supports the determinist excusal of responsibility, minimizing what might be called immoral acts to the level of necessary responses to stimuli and environment. Third and most important, Wright minimizes Bessie's murder with the implication that Bigger's discovery of self and freedom justifies or even necessitates the killing.

Margolies comments on the theme of Bigger's growth through this act of murder: "The monstrousness of the second murder exhilarates Bigger all the more. He has freely exercised his will--something he had never been able to do before. . . . His acts of murder are positive--thereby to a degree humanizing--since he is quite prepared to accept the consequences" (111). But Bigger's growth, while undeniable, is one-dimensional because it remains rooted in defiance and in the strange, untenable assertion of his still preserved moral purity; indeed, Wright goes so far as to suggest that Bigger does not discover his innocence or real self until he murders. As Brignano points out, Wright maintains throughout the novel a tone of virtual approval of the murder for its supposedly ultimate benefits to Bigger's consciousness:

> Wright implies that Bigger's killing of Mary is legitimate--the logical outcome of an acknowledged release from a consciously subservient group. "Normal" morality and law are suspended for Bigger, as Wright--through such means as the lawyer Max--forges the impression that a higher law justifies Bigger's deeds. Even the "immorality" of Bigger's subsequent murder of Bessie is complicated by the reader's feeling that Bigger has, for his own good, been set free from his former guilt and fear obsessions. He is now imbued with a manliness and pride of a new self. (35)

Bigger accepts responsibility for his crime only in an external sense, recognizing the predilection if not the right of society to take its revenge on him as it seems to have been doing, without apparent motivation, through his whole life. He does not recognize that he has done anything particularly reprehensible, but he does savor the fact that for the first time at least he has had some control over an action which will be taken seriously.

The persistent deterministic assumptions of the novel hold that the sociological cards have been stacked so heavily against Bigger that he has been forced to adopt this mode of expression of self and personality. But while Wright depicts Bigger's new freedom as metaphysically absolute, he ignores what Dostoevsky regards as the other, dialectical side of such a criminal's exploration--that in another sense the free man is now more a slave than ever. Although Bigger's quest for expression of personality is accomplished in an immediate sense, he heads rapidly toward self-destruction.

A good part of Wright's strategy in showing that Bigger feels no guilt over the murder of Bessie makes the sociological or deterministic point that Bigger's environment has so dehumanized him already as to make such a feeling impossible. Quite unlike Raskolnikov, Bigger does not feel even a momentary visitation of conscience over the murder. *Native Son* as a whole, and not just Bigger's reflections or viewpoint, notably lacks a sense of horror at the violation of the natural law and of the sacredness of life. In typical naturalistic fashion, Wright focuses on large, general, corporate sins such as the liberal Daltons' owning slum tenements, but fails to convey a strong conviction of the evil of certifiably evil acts--such as Bigger's beating in his lover's head with a brick. Immediately after throwing Bessie down the air shaft, Bigger reflects not on his culpability but on his stupidity for throwing the money down there with her: "Naw! He did not want to see her again. He felt that if he should ever see her face again he would be so overcome with a sense of guilt so deep as to be unbearable. That was a dumb thing to do, he thought. Throwing her away with all that money in her pocket" (224). But that potential sense of guilt remains only potential, for it is never heard from again or demonstrated as operating on Bigger in even an unconscious manner. Later, during his interrogation, in the only other reference to Bigger's thoughts about Bessie, we learn merely that "he had not thought of Bessie but once since his capture" (282). Not only Bigger, but Wright as well, pays little attention to the moral nature of the novel's most vicious act, presumably hoping to shock his audience into awareness of and sensitivity to their culpability. While Wright's inconsistent and essentially materialistic treatment of individual dignity in *Native Son* sets it contrary to *Crime and Punishment*, his novel displays some similar motifs and suggestions of direct influence from Dostoevsky's. In "How Bigger Was Born" Wright links Bigger generally with the modern revolt of the individual as seen in nineteenth-century Russia, indicating a familiarity with Russian history and literature:

> I was fascinated by the similarity of the emotional tensions of Bigger in America and Bigger in Nazi Germany and Bigger in old Russia. All Bigger Thomases, white and black, felt tense, afraid, nervous, hysterical, and restless. From far away Nazi Germany and old Russia had come to me items of knowledge that told me that certain modern experiences were creating types of personalities whose existence ignored racial and national lines of demarcation, that these personalities carried with them a more universal drama-element than anything I'd ever encountered before; that these personalities were mainly imposed upon men and women living in a world whose fundamental assumptions could no longer be taken for granted: a world ridden with national and class strife; a world whose metaphysical meanings had vanished; a world in which God no longer existed as a daily focal point of men's lives. (xix)

It is interesting that Wright does not develop the political implications of this unrest, but focuses on modern man's loss of metaphysical belief, the theme which is documented and analyzed throughout Dostoevsky's work.

Both *Crime and Punishment* and *Native Son* attain some of their highest tension immediately after the murder (or first killing, in Bigger's case). Parallel to Raskolnikov's terror behind the bolted door and his fortuitous escape from the building, is Bigger's fear as he stuffs Mary's body in the trunk and hauls her down to the furnace. His use of an axe to chop off her head reminds one of Raskolnikov's choice of murder weapon. When Bigger awakes suddenly from his first sleep after the killing, his shocked reflections, quite similar to Raskolnikov's, focus on the presence in his room of articles from the murder; he, too, goes out immediately and disposes of them. Bigger has a dream soon after the murder similar to Raskolnikov's of bludgeoning the pawnbroker repeatedly; but whereas Raskolnikov's dream suggests his horror and revulsion at taking another's life, Bigger's (of carrying around his own bloody, severed head in a package) focuses on the murder as his defiant act of self-destruction. Wright parallels Dostoevsky in showing his protagonist pushed to the limits of endurance after the killings by hunger, fear, and terrific tension. Wright, however, choosing not to represent guilt, whether unconscious or conscious, as one of those forces wearing down his protagonist, loses what in *Crime and Punishment* figures as the driving spiritual force effecting the killer's transformation. Wright echoes Raskolnikov's rejection of Sonya's cross when Bigger tears off the cross given him by the preacher; but while Raskolnikov eventually accepts both his literal and figurative cross, Bigger rejects once and for all not just the hatred of groups like the Ku Klux Klan but also all openness to religious belief. Wright substitutes his protagonist as a new Christ and new sacrificial victim: "His body seemed a flaming cross as words boiled hysterically out of him" (314).

In the controversial last third of *Native Son*, Wright's problems of artistic control and ideological consistency mar many of its earlier effects; but these problems at least point toward his more consistent (but still materialistic) treatment of collectivism-versus-individuality in *The Outsider*. Katherine Sprandel finds no contradiction in *Native Son*, claiming that Wright "deftly moves his hero out of the structures of naturalism into the freedom of existentialism. After demonstrating that whites are responsible for making

Bigger an outlaw and finally a murderer, Wright lifts Bigger out of this morass, permitting him to make an existential decision" (Ray 185). But such a view is untenable, for at the same time that Wright attempts to effect this transition to an existentialist theme, he continues to pound the reader with naturalistic and proletarian sermonizing. As Morris Dickstein comments, "Two-thirds of the way through the novel, it changes horses and devolves into a curious but inert essay on a novel that has essentially ended" (Ray 192). Margolies adds that

> The chief philosophical weakness of *Native Son* is not that Bigger does not surrender his freedom to Max's determinism, or that Bigger's Zarathustrian principles do not jibe with Max's socialist visions; it is that Wright himself does not seem to be able to make up his mind. There is an inconsistency of tone here--particularly in Book III, where the reader feels that Wright, although intellectually committed to Max's views, is more emotionally akin to Bigger's. (113)

Margolies also attacks the supposedly existential motivation of Bigger's acceptance of responsibility for Mary's death, pointing out Bigger's racial motivation: "He realizes he hates all whites with such an intensity that it gives him extreme pleasure to think that he had killed her deliberately" (115). Wright's attempt to include existentialist and personalist elements in the novel's latter stages foreshadows his future resolution of the dichotomy of collectivism versus individual freedom, evident in "The Man Who Lived Underground" and *The Outsider*. Speaking for Wright, the defense lawyer cites the denial of personality as society's main offense against Bigger and his forefathers, and he includes personality as one of the basic concepts of American civilization.

IV

The Outsider, undervalued by most critics and virtually dismissed by many, can be said to achieve greater power, complexity, and consistency than *Native Son*. With *The Outsider* Wright resolves the earlier novel's conflict between individual freedom and collectivism, stressing the former and attacking the latter as embodied in the American Communist Party. Although the later novel shows some ambivalence between self-will as a credo and its seductive, dangerous possibilities, Wright's emphasis on the individual's need for freedom remains consistent. And although there are echoes of the naturalistic agenda which clashes with the rising existentialism of *Native Son*, for the most part *The Outsider* satisfies with its development of a sophisticated analysis of revolt and retribution. Cross Damon has the opportunity to exercise his freedom much more than Bigger Thomas; he grows in parallel fashion but to a larger degree, gaining respect for himself by making choices rather than extorted promises. He accepts a nearly absolute freedom more intoxicating but also much more burdensome than either Bigger's freedom or his entrapment by environment and society. Thus Cross is a more complete existential hero than Bigger, facing not simply an unjust society but a meaningless universe, and creating his identity and values out of that void. Like Raskolnikov, Stavrogin, Ivan Karamazov, Fred Daniels, and the Invisible Man, Cross asserts his right-- even his duty--to test the moral universe.

Through Cross Wright takes the position of the reluctant agnostic or atheist, one who like Ivan Karamazov does not so much celebrate human freedom but insists that it be accepted and explored. Ivan reasons that "There is no virtue if there is no immortality" (60), concluding that "evil" actions are just as permissible as "good" ones. When Ivan finds that he is responsible for inciting his father's murder, he begins to reverse his unbelief through conversations with a devil. Cross remains similar to Ivan before the latter's painful transformation to belief, and Cross never sees the leap of faith as even a possibility. The narrator voices one of Wright's most crucial statements in *The Outsider*: "Damned is the man who must invent his own god" (360). For Wright the absence of God necessitates some sort of replacement; man has a duty to substitute some power or person, even oneself, as a source of values and identity. Like Kirilov of *The Devils*, Cross is a pioneer in this relatively new metaphysical world, which can acquire meaning only through the enthronement of individual will. But Kirilov's suicide, an act which is supposed to prove his perfect freedom and godhood, is interrupted by his mystical awakening, another change unlike Cross's unending revolt. Cross also reminds one of Stavrogin, who with conscious amorality determines to commit hideous acts in order to test himself to see if he can be revulsed by extremes of "evil" behavior. But whereas Stavrogin does recover his sense of good and evil just before his suicide, Cross's final horror upon dying is that he still feels innocent. Cross's name suggests several aspects of the paradox of freedom in need of restraint. His first name refers to his anger and to the burden he carries (as a modern Christ, or anti-Christ), which shifts from entrapment to freedom. He is a cross between the heroic and the demonic, and he symbolizes man's crossing over to the modern age, where the individual's acceptance of freedom sets him on potentially dangerous ground.

Unlike *Native Son*, where Wright alternates didactic praise and implied criticism of the Communist Party, *The Outsider* shows him consistently and virulently opposed to it, more explicitly on the grounds of human personality. In *The Devils* Dostoevsky uses Shatov to suggest his own defection (years before) from radical collectivism. He reveals leaders like Peter Verkhovensky as malicious, consciously despotic tyrants whose nominal commitment to human freedom is in fact hypocritical and overshadowed completely by their will to power. Shatov's deepening awareness of these violations of personality guides him to his heroic, sacrificial rejection of the radicals and to personal happiness. Wright's analysis of collectivism in *The Outsider* proceeds along similar lines (as does *Invisible Man*), focusing on collectivism's scorn for personal freedom and its arrogation of godlike control over people's lives and deaths. Unlike Shatov and the Invisible Man, however, Cross does not commit himself very deeply to the radicals, for he chooses to exploit them while he solidifies his identity. From his first acquaintance with Bob Hunter on the train to New York, Cross sees in the Party neither sincerity nor any relevance to his past life of enslavement or his present life of complete freedom. He uses the Party's manipulative tactics and its scorn for the individual against it, only seeming to be interested in its work. Wright confides his own skepticism about the sincerity of all political parties:

> Cross felt that at the heart of all political movements the concept of the basic inequality of man was enthroned and practiced, and the skill of politicians consisted in how cleverly they hid this elementary truth and gained votes by pretending the contrary. If, by pretending, he could find a hiding place, why, he could pretend that he believed in the Communist pretensions. (165)

Cross finds his suspicions of the Party confirmed in their betrayal and disposal of Bob, a devoted member who had put his faith in communism as the best hope for black people. Wright imputes to communists "a bad faith of which they were cynically proud" (187), claiming that they reject "from their hearts the pathos of living, purging their consciousness of that perilous subjective tension that spells the humanity of man" (188). The Party cynically arranged Eva Blount's marriage to the adulterous Gil to gain the prestige associated with her artwork, but ironically it refuses to recognize individual personality. When Gil is killed, the Party transforms him into a martyr and uses him as a theme for propaganda. With Cross's request that he simply be left alone by the communists, Wright echoes his own experience of being hounded and threatened as he drifted from Party influence. Wright summarizes his indictment of communism in claiming that its leaders do not believe in their own ideology, but only in the will to power (385). He finds both capitalism and communism guilty of "cheapening and devaluing our notions of human personality" (366). With Cross's murders of Herndon, Gil, and Hilton, Wright symbolically removes the evils of communism and fascism from existence. *The Outsider* does not feature a radical leader as chilling or as purely diabolical as Peter Verkhovensky or Jack from *Invisible Man*. But Wright, who made a more serious commitment to radicalism than either Dostoevsky or Ellison, reacts with noticeably greater vehemence with these symbolic executions.

Despite the lack of critical respect and attention paid to *The Outsider*, it succeeds as an exploration of ideas and as a novel of highly effective tension throughout, unlike *Native Son*, whose plot breaks down two-thirds of the way through in favor of various strains of rhetoric. *The Outsider* becomes Wright's more explicit echo of, and answer to *Crime and Punishment*, as he uses, with little transformation and striking liberality, several of the motifs, characters, and situations from Dostoevsky's novel. Both Raskolnikov and Cross have widowed, somewhat meddling mothers toward whom they feel both love and anger for expecting much of them. Both mothers have infused guilt and a neurotic self-image into their sons, who rebel against this moralism with nihilistic assertion of self. And both mothers see their sons as crosses they must bear and for whom they would sacrifice everything. Both young men are university dropouts in their early or mid-twenties who are crushingly poor but who feel that their superior intellect makes them superior to the masses of humanity. Like Bigger, Cross suffers from most of Raskolnikov's debilitating physical strains and tensions such as hunger, malnutrition, and even fever, which plays a large part in *Crime and Punishment*. But Wright's removal of guilt from Dostoevsky's scenario diminishes the intensity of his protagonist's suffering and his growth in self-knowledge. Wright uses two "Sonya" characters in his novel, the first being Jenny, the prostitute who offers to go away with Cross without knowing of his first murder. The second, Eva, though not a prostitute, is still a victim (of the Party) and hence possesses the understanding required to accept an outsider--to a certain degree. Wright offers Eva as Cross's Sonya, his one chance for salvation through risking total self-revelation. But Eva takes her own life, horrified at her lover's murder of her husband and others. She lacks Sonya's sense of herself as a sinner, and her moral naivete, suggested by her shock at discovering her own wishes for her husband's death, proves her undoing. Wright approves of Cross's risking all to abandon his proud, despairing and solitary life and to win Eva's trust and love.

Wright also includes a character much like Svidrigailov, whose function is similarly to suggest the protagonist's dual nature and to threaten him with his knowledge of the murders. Hilton, another cold-blooded amoralist, attempts to blackmail Cross out of desire for Eva, just as Svidrigailov seeks to use his knowledge to seduce Dunya. Cross momentarily recognizes Hilton's evil as part of himself, but kills him in an attempt to deny that evil or paradoxically to root it out: "Cross knew that the only difference between him and Hilton was that his demonism was not buttressed by ideas, a goal. So why should he care? But he did. And he hated Hilton as one can only hate something which is a part of one's own heart" (291). Wright uses Hilton's agnostic and nihilistic lecture to Cross just as Dostoevsky uses Svidrigailov's comments to enlarge Raskolnikov's self-knowledge; Hilton sounds just like Svidrigailov when the latter mocks idealism and discusses eternity as a room full of spiders:

> You're an inverted idealist. You're groping for some over-all concept to tie all life together. There is none, Lane.... Living in this world, Lane, is what we make it, and we make what there is of it. Beyond that there's nothing, nothing at all.... To think that there's something is foolish; to act as if there is something is mad. (*Outsider* 301)

Wright's clear borrowings from Dostoevsky extend to further elements of plot and character. One of the lesser but still obvious instances is his description of Cross's "wave of self-loathing" (56) and self-hatred that follows his leaving the university, in direct correlation to Raskolnikov's attitude upon leaving his studies. As will be discussed below, the relationship between Cross and the detective Ely Houston parallels almost exactly that between Raskolnikov and Porfiry (the only significant difference being that Wright's detective does not face his intuitive knowledge that Cross is the murderer). Cross's bolting up in bed and remembering the bloody handkerchief clearly recalls Raskolnikov's identical action over his bloody trouser fringes and stolen items. Wright exempts Cross from the rationalism which infects Raskolnikov, but he describes Cross's entrapment in words that closely approximate Dostoevsky's about thought taking the place of life: "His damned habit of relentless thinking was mangling the very tendons and nerves of the flesh of life!" (327). Suggesting that Cross considers suicide, Wright offers as motivation his haughty pride and his feeling of superiority over others, both reasons which tempt Raskolnikov to do the same: "The shame of having to tell, to explain to strangers, would be overpowering. That could not happen; he would make use of his gun on himself first" (330). And the scene where Cross confesses his murders to Eva recalls Raskolnikov's confession to Sonya and his discovery of new life in Siberia, especially when Cross falls to his knees, "clutching his arms about her legs" (397).

Ely Houston, the detective who understands Cross's rebellious, nihilistic impulses and suspects him of murder, is a direct but somewhat inert copy of Porfiry Petrovich, who hounds Raskolnikov and points out to him the inevitability of either confession or suicide. The major critics of Wright's work, when they comment at all on this connection (or any between these two novels), restrict themselves to general, brief, minimal observations of a certain similarity. Margolies, for example, says only that Houston "reminds one of the cunning, intellectual and psychological Porfiry" (137). But while Wright provides Houston with slight touches of Porfiry's acuity and psychological perspicuity, his character remains relatively flat and unconvincing, lacking his alter ego's charm and irony. Houston does not attain full knowledge of Cross's guilt until the end because Wright wishes to accentuate the bold, superior aspect of Cross in accepting his freedom and creating his own values. Houston, however, shares Porfiry's understanding of the dark impulses of human nature and of the criminal's need for punishment:

> My position's difficult. I feel outside the lives of men. Yet my job demands that I enforce the law against the outsider who breaks the law. . . . My greatest sympathy is for those who feel that they have a *right* to break the law. . . . Most of them almost beg you to punish them. They would be lost without the law. (*Outsider* 134)

Porfiry's insight is quite similar, and he too shares some feelings with the murderer: ''I can understand what it must be for a man like you to have brought all this on himself. . . . I am acquainted with all these feelings, and I read your article with a sense of familiarity'' (381). Wright lifts intact the whole motif of the cat-and-mouse game between the detective who has his own peculiar but astute psychological or historical analyses, and the criminal who tries in vain to disguise his vexation and discomfiture.

At moments the reader of *The Outsider* might wonder whether he is reading an explicit adaptation of Dostoevsky's novel, as when Cross wonders to himself:

> Was Houston raising the question of the Negro to mislead him before he was told that he was under arrest? Why didn't he come right out with what he wanted? He had a foolish desire to reach forward and grab Houston's shoulder and say to him: All right, I know you're after me. . . . Let's get it over with. (128)

Wright gives to Houston Porfiry's winking, his clipped phrasing, his light, bantering tone calculated to ease the suspect into feeling comfortable, and his love of springing surprises on the suspect to force a breakdown of his defenses. Houston duplicates Porfiry's confidential tone used to convince the criminal of the detective's sincerity: ''What kind of motive could such a killer have? That's what's puzzling me'' (280). Wright's appropriation of motifs and ideas here even extends to the use of Porfiry's ''psychological proof'' and the comparison of the killer to Napoleon, which becomes one of Porfiry's recurring themes. As Houston says,

> The proof is easy to see, but it is a rather daring kind of proof. Of course, this kind of proof cannot be introduced into court. It has a psychological basis. It's an "as if" proof. . . . It's an intuition; it must first come from your own heart, see? How do I know that all three men feel alike? I know because *I* feel that way. (283)

Wright also patterns the final interview between Cross and Houston after that of Raskolnikov and Porfiry, emphasizing at this point the fundamentally compassionate, even brotherly concern of the detective for the criminal. Just as Porfiry drops all pretense of ambiguity and advises Raskolnikov to confess in order to avoid suicide, Houston points out the retributive torment Cross supposedly will undergo in freedom if he does not confess: "You made your own law. And, by God, I, for one, am going to let you live by it. . . . You are going to punish yourself, see? You are your own law, so you'll be your own judge" (429). But while Porfiry says that Raskolnikov probably will find his way back to humanity and to life, Houston predicts that Cross will not.

Another work of Russian literature to which *The Outsider* evidently makes indirect reference is Gogol's "The Overcoat," one of the seminal works of nineteenth-century Russian fiction. Gogol's story also presents a lower-level civil servant and his struggle with issues of human dignity and identity in a cramping environment. Akaky Akakievich allows society to devalue him because of his poverty, and his new confidence after acquiring a beautiful new coat shatters when it is stolen from him. Wright places an unusual amount of emphasis on Cross's overcoat throughout Book One, suggesting it as a similar symbol of selfhood and changeable identity. But while Akaky identifies so much with the new self that his coat seems to provide, he shows the weakness of that self when the coat is removed. Cross on the other hand, relying on internal strength rather than on external trappings, does not mind parting with his overcoat as a symbol of his former self; indeed, the loss of the coat in the train wreck makes possible his new life. Before the wreck, Cross has his gun in the coat, suggesting his need for feelings of power and manhood. After he accidentally leaves the overcoat (but not the gun) in the train, he finds his clothes free of blood; his overcoat "had protected him somewhat" (78), as Akaky feels his coat does. Cross's postal badge and loan papers left behind in the overcoat seem to establish a dead man on the train as Cross Damon. On Cross's first morning of freedom, he shops for a new overcoat "and other necessities" (91), for he needs to choose a whole new identity. When he stealthily goes to his old neighborhood, he uses the new overcoat to disguise himself (just as the Invisible Man does with his "Rinehart" glasses). Upon arriving in Harlem Cross observes a depressing scene reminiscent of Gogol's story, with defeated masses of people "huddled in overcoats, trudging through snowy streets" (137). Akaky does attempt an original, almost rebellious act of personality when he reports the theft to his superior and complains of bureaucratic delay. But his essential instability cannot withstand the furious response of his division chief, and he dies soon after. A dramatic and pivotal passage of the story states that "In all his life he had never been so severely reprimanded by a high official. . . . He walked open-mouthed through a blizzard, again and again stumbling off the sidewalk" (92). Wright approximates this description to show his protagonist on the contrary rejecting passivity and seizing his opportunity for rebirth: "He was stunned and shaken by the power of an idea that took his breath away and left him standing open-mouthed like an idiot amid the crazy flakes" (82). Thus Cross reverses the direction taken by Gogol's Akaky Akakievich by beginning his creative rebellion out of his "death."

Although there are some important differences between *The Outsider* and *Crime and Punishment*, one can trace their relationship of thematic influence and/or consistency in several areas. First and most basic, Wright extends Dostoevsky's observation on the need for self-assertion even if it ends disastrously. Dostoevsky reserves some respect and admiration for Raskolnikov, Kirilov, Stavrogin, and Ivan for their determination to pursue their ideas to their logical if dangerous conclusions. As Ivan notes in his tale of the Grand Inquisitor, many people lack the courage to accept freedom, preferring the comfort and security of strict prescriptions of their behavior and thinking. Ivan's Inquisitor rebukes Christ for giving man the alluring but insupportable burden of freedom:

> But what happened? Instead of taking man's freedom from them, Thou didst make it greater than ever! Didst Thou forget that man prefers peace, and even death to freedom of choice in the knowledge of good and evil? Nothing is more seductive for man than his freedom of conscience, but nothing is a greater cause of suffering. (235)

Bob Hunter of *The Outsider* illustrates this tendency of the weak individual to escape into the certitude and order of authoritarian collectivism, which denies his humanity and cruelly discards him. Cross sees that Sarah's desire to return to the church at the end of the novel constitutes a betrayal of self and freedom: ''Poor Sarah. . . she was crushed and scared. She had to rest, to find support, a master; she was yearning to submit. . . . She did not want the responsibility of her life any longer. Why was life given if man could not handle it?'' (413, 414). Wright indicates that Eva's tears at her husband's funeral are caused not by grief but by her fear of being on the verge of an unsettling freedom. Cross, on the other hand, is called to a radical freedom, and he does not flinch from the potential terror of the calling.

A second connection between these novels is the dread of such inner investigations. Through most of *Crime and Punishment* Raskolnikov bitterly rejects conscious guilt while he examines his seemingly illogical suffering. And Svidrigailov is transformed from a bored aesthete to a man who recognizes and regrets his evil after a night full of profoundly troubling dreams. Although Wright for the most part underscores Cross's innocence (in contrast to Dostoevsky's demonstration of Raskolnikov's guilt), he does include a dialectical consideration of Cross's inner darkness. The epigraph to Book One, from Kierkegaard, suggests that Cross not only desires freedom and a fuller identity, but also fears them: "Dread is an alien power which lays hold of an individual, and yet one cannot tear oneself away, nor has a will to do so; for one fears what one desires" (1). Cross's train ride to New York signifies a journey within, and he fears what he might discover:

> As the train wheels clicked through the winter night, he knew where his sense of dread came from; it was from within himself, within the vast and mysterious world that was his and his alone, and yet not really known to him, a world that was his own and yet unknown. And it was into this strange but familiar world that he was now plunging. (117)

In contrast to Cross, who welcomes the chance to look within, Eva denies her feelings of guilt over wishing for her husband's death; she jumps to her death out of a failure to accept not just Cross's but also her own culpability. And Ely Houston shrinks from his intuitive knowledge of Cross's guilt out of a reluctance to acknowledge his own potential for just such brutality.

Late in the novel Wright develops one aspect of his ambivalent position on self-will, namely the idea that Cross has made himself as monstrous as those oppressors whom he had sought to remove. This third similarity to *Crime and Punishment* emerges in Cross's reflection (quoted above) that he is virtually as demonic as Hilton, the coldest of the communists. Further strains of "The Grand Inquisitor" are heard in Cross's discussion with Blimin, as he attacks capitalism and communism because they enslave humanity. Yet his thesis, a clear paraphrase of the Inquisitor's, holds that since men fear freedom, the strong who accept it have a right and duty to control humanity:

> Those few strong men who do not want to be duped, and who are stout enough in their hearts to accept a godless world, are quite willing, aye, anxious to let the masses of men rest comfortably in their warm cocoons of traditional illusions.... The slaves of today are those who are congenitally afraid of the new and the untried, who fall on their knees and break into a deep sweat when confronted with the horrible truth of the uncertain and enigmatic nature of life....

It is the strong at the top, however, who represent modern man.
Beyond themselves, their dreams, their hopes, their plans, they
know that there is nothing. (361)

Thus although Cross despises the cynical masters of the world, he becomes like
them in the exploitation and elimination of others. He finds himself becoming
a "little god," like the hated Gil, Herndon, and Hilton. Raskolnikov's dream
in Siberia of a world of madmen and murderers infected by rationalist ideas
makes him recoil finally from his claim of the right to kill. But although Cross
can be disturbed momentarily by what he has become, he never surrenders
his "innocence" because in his view he has transcended all moral boundaries.

A fourth point of compatibility between Wright and Dostoevsky comes in
the character of Ely Houston as a statement on the voluntary limits of freedom,
and in Cross's horror at his "innocence." Like Ivan, Houston shares Cross's
insights on God and on man's freedom to transgress all laws; he also shares
Cross's urges to create his own values, to dedicate himself to self-will, and to
become a virtual god who exercises power over others: "Houston was a district
attorney sworn to uphold a system of law in which he did not really believe.
Houston was an impulsive criminal who protected himself against himself by
hunting down other criminals" (137). Porfiry Petrovich, in contrast to Houston,
understands but does not agree with Raskolnikov's justification of murder. He
tries to lead Raskolnikov to see his need for a spiritual renewal. Houston's
position as district attorney allows him to relish his power over other transgres-
sors, but he stops short of actual revolt, contenting himself with philosophical
and psychological rebellion. As Houston says to Cross, "A lawless man has to
rein himself in. A man of lawless impulses living in a society which seeks to
restrain instinct for the common good must be in a kind of subjective prison.
How such a man must live and sweat behind the bars of himself" (282).
Houston and Ivan Karamazov authorize but do not actually commit any
transgression, while Cross and Smerdyakov reason and then act out their
murders. (Cross, however, unlike the lackey Smerdyakov, does not derive or

borrow his theory from anyone.) Houston holds two contrary meanings for Wright: first, Houston lacks something of Cross's courage and heroic stature because he fails to recognize himself in the mirror of Cross and because he balks at truly asserting his freedom. But second, Wright uses Houston in a positive sense, indicating his voluntary restriction of self-will as a means of sanity and survival.

When Cross dies he makes a troubling and ambiguous statement about the horror he has discovered: "Because in my heart . . . I'm . . . I felt . . . I'm innocent. . . . That's what made the horror" (440). Unlike Dostoevsky's protagonists as well as Fred Daniels and the Invisible Man, Cross finds no limits, no revulsion for what he has done. He has glimpsed and acted out the possibilities of unlimited freedom, and found them seductive. He has killed repeatedly and in cold blood, yet finds nothing with which to reproach himself. He finds horror not in his actions per se, but in his supposed innocence, in his license. Wright implies that he finds Cross less than totally innocent. Like Cross, he seems to regret the absoluteness of the freedom that man can discover. Wright's view of freedom differs somewhat from Dostoevsky's, but at times Wright also implies that man needs to set a limit on his self-assertion to be happy or even to survive.

In contrast to these areas of thematic and philosophical agreement between *Crime and Punishment* and *The Outsider*, their significant differences stem from Wright's ambivalence on self-assertion and his variable reluctance to devalue it, even when faced with the individual's monstrousness and self-destruction. As in *Native Son*, Wright again performs a materialistic analysis of individualism, freedom, and revolt, as opposed to Dostoevsky's and Ellison's metaphysical or spiritual analyses, which mount a more cogent and consistent defense of the nonmaterial values of freedom and dignity. *Native Son*'s promulgation of self-assertion intensifies and becomes more explicit in *The Outsider*, as the focus shifts from man's escape from entrapment to his need to exercise as high a degree of freedom as possible. Although through this self-assertion man discovers more than ever how "meaningless" existence is, the activity itself gives man the power to confer values while it also becomes a kind of value, or all-important source of meaning. Because of this significance of self-will in Wright's schema, he tends to condone or minimize some of its excesses. For he points out that Bigger's and now Cross's spectacular growth in freedom and the creative choice of one's self is made possible only through what society sees as the criminal assertion of self. As discussed in the treatment of *Native Son*, this idea of Wright's can be traced to the body of Dostoevsky's work. But Wright's wish to move his audience toward either social justice (*Native Son*) or existential awareness (*The Outsider*), together with his evident agnosticism, leaves his protagonists without a stage of self-surrender, and without peace or fulfillment. To Dmitry Karamazov's agonized question of how man is going to be good without God, Wright has no answer.

Wright does reverse the thesis of *Crime and Punishment* insofar as he develops a protagonist who succeeds in Raskolnikov's attempt to dispel his conscience and find no limit to his right of self-assertion. Raskolnikov succumbs to the weakening of his physical and mental faculties during and after the murders, contrary to his theory that as an exceptional individual he is exempt from this decline and the effects of conscience. Cross, however, only grows stronger in his resolve, shrewdness, and rejection of guilt over the course of his four murders. Before the murder of Joe, he asserts an innocence about himself which allows him alone to judge his actions: "There was a kind of innocence that made him want to shape for himself the kind of life he wanted, but he knew that that innocence was deeply forbidden. In a debate with himself that went on without words, he asked himself if one had the right to such an attitude. Well, he would see" (86). After the murder, he refines this idea and feels the weight of this evolving existentialism:

> Cross had to discover what was good or evil through his own actions, which were more exacting than the edicts of any God because it was he alone who had to bear the brunt of their consequences with a sense of absoluteness made intolerable by

knowing that this life of his was all he had and would ever have. (123)

He takes solace in jazz and the blues, "the musical language of the satisfiedly amoral, the boastings of the contentedly lawless, the recreations of the innocently criminal" (140).

Cross experiences no stirrings of conscience or guilt over the murders, never wondering if he has the moral right to do as he does. His mother induced in him early in life a general, primordial sense of guilt about his very existence, and she tried "to teach him to be his own judge" (20). A fundamental aspect of Cross's rebellion, similar to Raskolnikov's, is his resentful rejection of his mother and this neurotic, internalized guilt. In a direct echo of the letter of Raskolnikov's mother, Cross's mother pressures him about his evident atheism: "I need to know that you've found God, Cross. . . . For months now everything I've heard about you is bad" (23). Cross does teach himself to be his own judge, but he reverses his mother's intent by asserting his basic innocence. Wright points out that high-pitched moralism often creates individuals who are profoundly amoral and capable of anything: "This blue-jazz was a rebel art blooming seditiously under the condemnations of a Protestant ethic just as his own consciousness had sprung conditioned to defiance from his relationship to his mother, who had shrilly evoked in him exactly what she had so desperately tried to smother" (140). Thus Wright implicitly indicts many if not most religious individuals for creating the Cross Damons by planting the seeds of such revolt with their strict, joyless moralizing. After Cross pushes Joe out of the eighth-floor window to his death, he does not feel regret or guilt but only relief that this obstacle to his new life has been removed. After bashing in the skulls of Herndon and Gil, "There was no regret for what he had done; no, none at all" (230). Speaking to Eva near the novel's end, Cross in fact posits the rightness of the murders, claiming that his private ethics overrule morality: "I kept hitting them until they were dead. . . . I was not sorry. . . . I know I was right" (400). At moments Cross does feel guilt, but never over the murders; his infused guilt reappears but in weakened form: "It was not a guilt for his having murdered; it was because he now saw that he held over the life of Eva a godlike power and knowledge that even Gil or the Party had not held" (237). His power over Eva fills him sometimes with guilt, sometimes with intense pleasure. Cross regrets some of the consequences of his actions, however, if not the actions themselves. First, he reluctantly begins to acknowledge that he is becoming more like these "little gods" he has removed. And second, he feels regret and "self-loathing" (406) after Eva's suicide, not because his actions were wrong but because she found them so horrifying and because they have cost him her love. Although, or perhaps because Cross does not feel any guilt over the murders, he can recognize and exploit repressed guilt in others. He sees that Eva's fantasy of seeing Herndon on the stairs with a gun springs from her guilt over wishing for her husband's death, and he uses this guilt to protect himself. Her guilt over wanting to kill Hilton also blinds her to Cross's culpability. Houston also retreats for a long time from the clear psychological evidence before him indicating that Cross is the murderer because Houston does not wish to admit his own similar capacity.

Part of Wright's didactic intent in *The Outsider* is to show the individual freeing himself through self-assertion, and in this respect Wright develops Cross as a character with some heroic qualities. Because of this purpose, Wright at times tends to minimize Cross's responsibility for the murders, and he does much to deflect the reader's possible antipathy for the murderer by concentrating on the evil of most of murdered. Although *The Outsider* for the most part proposes a predominantly anti-naturalistic thesis, in places it indulges in a commingling of naturalistic implications reminiscent of *Native Son*. Wright may have had difficulty ridding himself completely of this attitude which informs his early fiction; through most of *The Outsider* it seems to be superseded by Cross's new freedom, only to reassert itself subtly in the latter section of the novel. A strong sense of entrapment pervades the first part of the novel, as Cross feels intensely the need to escape the people and environmental

124

circumstances which make his life unbearable. Wright emphasizes Cross's victimization by heredity with commentary on his mother's gifts to him of dread and morbid reflection. Her incessant preaching has brought about in him ''an unbridled hunger for the sensual'' and has deformed him by making him ''instinctively choose to love himself over and against all others because he felt himself menaced by a mysterious God Whose love seemed somehow like hate'' (18). Cross feels danger closing in on him as his girlfriend threatens to throw him in jail for statutory rape and his wife refuses a divorce and demands a huge sum of money. His wish for flight and escape calls to mind the feelings of Bigger Thomas and several characters from *Uncle Tom's Children*. After Cross finds release in his ''death'' and new life, his creative exploration of freedom dissipates the naturalistic focus. But the idea of Cross as a victim of environment, carefully established by Wright, persists and tends to mitigate Cross's culpability for the murder of Joe; indeed, this first murder seems a necessary response if not of self-defense then at least of preservation: ''He had had no other choice; it had been either he or Joe'' (111). Wright reverts to a vaguely naturalistic motif later with the observation that Cross has become enmeshed in compulsive acts of violence which he would rather stop, ''hating that part of himself that he could not manage'' (346). This desire to stop surely humanizes Cross, showing his recognition on some level of the evil; but he continues to choose self-will and to murder whomever he wishes. The depiction of Cross as controlled by his excesses conflicts with the fundamental theme of freedom and denies him some of the responsibility for his actions which he seeks so passionately. A passage from *The House of the Dead* describes precisely the exultation of a man like Cross whose revolt against moral law initiates an intoxicating but morbid and ominous new life of freedom:

> Now here is where the strangeness sets in: for a time the man suddenly breaks all bounds.... It is as though, once having leaped beyond the boundary that was sacred for him, he now began to

revel in the fact that nothing was sacred for him any more, as
though he felt an urge at one bound to leap beyond all law and
authority and to enjoy the thrill of horror which he could hardly not
feel toward himself. He knows, moreover, that a terrible punishment awaits him. (148)

After the murder of Joe, Cross advances swiftly toward the other murders as
further discovery and proof of his freedom.

Although Wright does give some attention to the demonic aspect of Cross's
adventures, he renders three of the four murders with a tone bordering on
positive sympathy because they figure for Wright as symbolic executions of the
enslavers of mankind. When Cross decides to pursue ultimate freedom after the
train wreck, Wright underlines his courage and innocence, claiming that his
criminality consists more of a rebellious feeling than of any action:

All his life he had been hankering after his personal freedom, and
now freedom was knocking at his door, begging him to come in.
. . . In a way, he was a criminal, not so much because of what he
was doing, but because of what he was feeling. It was for much
more than merely criminal reasons that he was fleeing to escape
his identity, his old hateful consciousness. (84, 86)

The tone of qualified innocence continues through Joe's murder and the
ideological killings of the "insects" Gil, Herndon, and Hilton, whereby Wright
avenges himself on the purveyors of his former illusions about collectivism and
its promises. In setting forth his expose of the Party's cruel exploitation of
powerless people, Wright parallels the legend of the Grand Inquisitor by
emphasizing the cynicism of the masters as well as the masses' weakness and
longing for some figure to give them security in exchange for freedom. Gil
Blount and Jack Hilton symbolize the Party's cold inhumanity and passion for
control of others, similar to that of Peter Verkhovensky of *The Devils* and Jack
of *Invisible Man*. With Cross's unpremeditated but gratuitous murders of
Herndon and Gil, Wright abandons the motif of self-preservation established
with Joe's murder and lends a strong tone of approval to his protagonist's

removal of two emblems of authoritarianism. Cross kills Herndon and Gil largely out of revulsion at their fascistic and communistic attempts to exercise their "will to power" (385). After the murders Cross implies to Eva that his motives were not personal as much as ideological. The ideological thrust of his motivation, however, threatens to render these murders less concrete for the reader and therefore less horrifying and possibly less objectionable. Cross feels a mixture of aesthetic disgust with, and moral superiority over the two men, and these feelings encourage his standing in judgment over them. After Cross kills Herndon, the narrator notes that "the imperious feeling that had impelled him to action was not fulfilled. His eyes were unblinkingly on Gil's face. Yes, this other insect had to be crushed, blotted out of existence" (226). Wright extends the tone of qualified acceptance of violence with the murder of Hilton, who is more monstrous than Herndon or Gil. Cross kills Hilton partly to protect himself and partly to avenge those like Bob Hunter who have been victims of the Party. The juxtaposition of Hilton's evil and Cross's nobility in acting for others tends to deflect the reader's potential antipathy for this cold-blooded execution. In an attempt to humanize his increasingly inhuman protagonist, Wright notes that in the seconds before Cross kills Hilton he has to choke off momentary impulses of compassion and restraint. But whereas Cross kills Herndon and Gil in immediate flashes of anger and revulsion, he commits this murder with cold premeditation, arrogating to himself the right to decide who has and who has not the right to live.

Wright further mitigates the sense of Cross's culpability with the observation that his fundamental crime in the eyes of society is not the taking of life but asserting a freedom and a new self that does not recognize conventional human law:

> He knew that he had cynically scorned, wantonly violated, every commitment that civilized men owe, in terms of common honesty and sacred honor, to those with whom they live. That, in essence, was his crime. The rest of his brutal and bloody thrashings about

were the mere offshoots of that one, central, cardinal fact. (374)

Cross is offered as an intellectual and existential superman who sees through the deceptions foisted upon the common man: "The only real enemies of this system are not the rats themselves, but those outsiders who are conscious of what is happening and who seek to change the consciousness of the rats who are being controlled" (363). The reference to Cross's situation as the "dilemma of the ethical criminal" (346), which might be rendered more precisely if strangely as the "dilemma of the ethical murderer," summarizes Wright's defense of his protagonist as one who responds to a law higher than that against murder. But Wright weakens his novel's defense of human freedom and dignity to the extent that he exonerates Cross's violations of others' right to live.

Wright shows the influence of Dostoevsky in focusing on atheism as the primary cause of the decay of values and order in the modern world. With *Crime and Punishment*, *The Devils*, and *The Brothers Karamazov* Dostoevsky analyzes man's loss of belief as the gravest danger to the individual and the community. But while Dostoevsky both explores the darkness of unbelief and depicts regeneration through the beginning of faith, Wright does not make the transition, leaving his protagonists stranded in their atheistic and nihilistic revolt. Paraphrasing a key point made in *The Devils*, Houston aligns Cross with atheists whose revolt is radical and fearsome: "It is only when they don't feel the need to deny Him that they really don't believe in Him. . . . *You went all the way*! You have drawn all the conclusions and deductions that could be drawn from the atheistic position and you have inherited the feelings that only real atheists can have" (424). The district attorney finds in Cross "the return of ancient man, pre-Christian man," who is guided by "nothing at all but his own desires, which would be his only values" (316). Dostoevsky has sympathy for the atheist (Raskolnikov, Stavrogin, Kirilov, Ivan) because of his suffering and the earnestness of his struggle for truth. Wright bases his sympathy for the atheist on these factors but also on a shared disillusionment with, and even hostility toward faith and religion. *The Outsider* extends the idea implicit in

Native Son that belief is for the weak and/or hypocritical. Bigger rejects the consolations of religion offered by his mother and the preacher as false, a betrayal of the courageous new self he has chosen; the mob's burning the cross outside his cell proves to him that religion is based on fear and hatred. Cross's anger toward his mother's guilt-ridden faith emerges when he burns the church with the draft records office in the basement. In analyzing modern atheism and belief, Cross portrays the image of God as a sort of superstition, a fearful projection of human need:

> It means that God no longer really concerns us as a reality beyond life, but simply as something projected compulsively from men's minds in answer to their chronic need to be rid of fear, something to meet the obscure needs of daily lives lived amidst strange and threatening facts. (359)

For Cross, the absence of God translates into the idea that, whether fortunately or unfortunately, we "can do what we damn well please on this earth" (360). Reflecting on Sarah's surrender of her freedom for religious comfort, the narrator expresses Wright's lament that this behavior is passed on through generations:

> All the church had to do was predict that life would be terrible, that men would become overwhelmed with contradictory experiences. They could drill this simple, elementary truth of life into the hearts of impressionable children. Then the fathers of the church could sit back and watch the generations of the sons and daughters of men grow up and go forth on their little voyages of proud, vain desire, could watch them with soft, ironic smiles, for they knew that sooner or later they would come crawling back to the faith of their childhood, seeking solace, wanting mercy, forgiveness. (415)

(As Cross mocks Sarah in saying that perhaps God uses the devil to guide people to truth, he paraphrases the devil's comment to the unbelieving Ivan Karamazov.) Wright's generally negative attitude toward belief adds a sympathetic background to Cross's revolt and repudiation of conventional moral values. Although Houston keeps his own nihilistic impulses in check, he shares with Cross an atheistic world-view and the insight that Cross's real crime is his assertion of absolute freedom based on that view. If society were aware of the depth of Cross's revolt, it would feel threatened that he might infect others and reveal that modern man has already lost God but simply has not realized or admitted it yet.

Dostoevsky often depicts the rebel achieving his identity through reconnection with the community. In *The Outsider*, however, Wright tends to elevate one's responsibility to himself over responsibility to others, sometimes favoring the former when it seems to conflict with the latter. Similar to the superfluous man of nineteenth-century Russian fiction, Cross displays an apparent shiftlessness which disguises a hunger for real responsibility which has been denied by society:

> What had irked him about his past responsibilities had been their dullness, their tenuity, their tendency simply to bore him. What he needed, demanded, was the hardest, the most awful responsibility, something that would test him and make him feel his worth. And his South Side Chicago environment had held forth no hope of his ever being able to find any such responsibility. (143)

He hates his old life because its responsibilities consisted of extorted promises which denied him freedom. Therefore Cross celebrates his escape from the impingement of false duties, wondering how one can respect others while living in such a void:

> If he was to be loyal, to love, to show pity, mercy, forgiveness, if he was to abstain from cruelty, to be mindful of the rights of others ... how was it to be done so that the carrying out of these duties and the practicing of these virtues in the modern world would not reduce a healthy, hungry man to a creature of nervous dread. (376)

Yet as his freedom opens up a world of stunning possibilities, Cross experiences momentarily a need for connection with other people. This need deepens in his relationship with Eva, for he wishes to make to her the first free promise

of his life. As with Sonya in *Crime and Punishment*, Eva represents the
protagonist's potential link back to humanity. Cross confesses everything to
her and begins telling the truth when a simple lie (about his motive for killing
her husband) would have kept her from suicide. He does this out of a strong
sense of responsibility to himself which has Wright's sympathy but which
overrules the risk to Eva. This act of self-revelation is more egotistical and self-
righteous than loving, and it destroys her. Eva's fall from a building ironically
parallels the murder of Joe and makes her Cross's last, though unintended
victim.   At the moments in the novel when Cross implies a belief in
responsibility to others, his words sound hollow and forced, contradicted by his
entire psychology and behavior. He hints of social duty when he tells the
communist Blimin that a man should face the "horrible totalitarian reptile"
and warn others of "its multitudinous writhings" (367). But Wright awkwardly has his own didactic message of social concern come from a man who
does not care about other people. When Cross dies, his expressed regret about
remaining alone and not making meaningful connections with others belies his
proud isolation and his continued assertions that he is an innocent murderer.

Although for the most part *The Outsider* stresses the innocence of Cross
Damon, in places it echoes *Crime and Punishment*'s observation that the
criminal often expects or needs punishment to atone for his wrongs. Cross
surprises one with his feeling of terror when Houston abandons him to his
freedom:

> The prop had gone; Houston had gone; the world against which he
> had pitched his rebellion had pitied him, almost forgiven him. . .
> . He was not to be punished! Men would not give meaning to what
> he had done! Society would not even look at it, recognize it! That
> was not fair, wasn't right, just. (431)

However, Cross feels the need for punishment not because he finds his actions
unlawful or immoral, but because his freedom has become such a torment after
the suicide of Eva. With Houston's comment that Cross will judge and punish

himself, Wright implies some compunction in Cross, but he shows no evidence of this feeling in his character. By killing off his protagonist Wright loses any chance for Cross to renounce his "innocence," and the novel loses an ending which might have been both more troubling and more hopeful--Cross walking the streets, utterly free and alone to reconstruct himself again and to live with his memories. Wright saves Cross from a protracted period of suffering, but in so doing he denies him a retributive awakening and a discovery that he is not beyond good and evil. With the murder of Cross by the communists and his final declaration of innocence, Wright attempts to evoke a final sympathy for him in order to mitigate the reader's possible revulsion at the murders and even to suggest Cross's martyrdom in the cause of accepting the burden of freedom.

Chapter 4

Creative Revolt and Responsibility:
The Devils, *The Brothers Karamazov*, "The Man Who Lived Underground," and *Invisible Man*

I

Chapters One and Two discussed the early work of Dostoevsky, Wright, and Ellison, emphasizing first each writer's sympathy with the deterministic or naturalistic viewpoint, and then each writer's growing dissatisfaction with that explanation of human behavior and with radical collectivism. Chapter Three analyzed Dostoevsky's influence on Wright's evolving anti-collectivism, focusing on their agreement in several areas as well as their debate on the limits and purpose of self-will. This chapter treats the further influence of Dostoevsky on both Wright and Ellison by examining all three writers' most comprehensive critiques of naturalism and collectivism and their shared positive ideal of individual responsibility to others which can issue from creative revolt. Of Dostoevsky's works, *Notes from Underground* and *The Brothers Karamazov* exerted the most influence on "The Man Who Lived Underground" and *Invisible Man*, with *The Devils* connecting as well to Ellison's novel. The two American writers look to *Notes from Underground* for the basic metaphor of the protagonist's seeking shelter "underground" while hoping for strength enough to rise to new life; they look to *The Brothers Karamazov* with their depiction of underground men as non-neurotic individuals capable of accepting responsibility for their freedom and serving others.

The Devils analyzes the suffering of several individuals, Stavrogin, Shatov, and Kirilov, who struggle in roundabout fashions through self-assertion and ultimately toward self-denial. Not so narrowly political nor so didactically reactionary a novel as many critics have seen it, *The Devils* concerns itself with anarchism not solely for its frightful political implications for Russia, but for the underlying, and far more devastating spiritual vacuum of relativism which it reveals. Dostoevsky demonstrates the logical and inevitable declension from the superfluity of the generation of the forties through the materialistic nihilism of the sixties and the amoral relativism and revolutionism of the early seventies. He finds paradoxically that it is precisely these individuals who presume to have gone beyond good and evil that come the closest to discovery of an intense faith. In *The Brothers Karamazov* Dostoevsky attacks materialism and atheism more explicitly than in *Crime and Punishment* or *The Devils*. He presents Ivan as another man who, like Stavrogin, tests the idea that there is neither good nor evil and who experiences a type of conversion through an anguished discovery of personal responsibility for a crime of which he is innocent legally but not morally. The other apparently innocent brothers, Dmitry and Alyosha, also learn of individual and universal culpability, each finding an ecstatic union with all suffering people. With this novel Dostoevsky adds an element not present in *Crime and Punishment* or *The Devils*: the positive ideal of active love, demonstrated in the words of Father Zosima and in the actions of all three brothers, each of whom undergoes a change from self-assertion to self-denial.

"The Man Who Lived Underground," published in 1945, five years after *Native Son* and eight years before *The Outsider*, links with the novels in some respects while it stands apart from them in others. Although it does not deal explicitly with collectivism, it shows Wright's growing interest in individual experience over political involvement. It clarifies the somewhat ambiguous anti-naturalism of *Native Son* by exploring a protagonist's range of freedom which is much larger than that of Bigger Thomas but not yet so absolute as that of Cross Damon. It also extends the theme of freedom as an opportunity *and* a burden, for Fred Daniels shares with Bigger and Cross the heroic aspect of accepting such a challenge. Yet "The Man Who Lived Underground" displays more consistency on the idea of self-will than either of the novels, both of which alternately endorse and devalue it. In the two major novels Wright is seen to be much more reluctant than Dostoevsky to withdraw support from his characters' nihilistic tendencies. This story lacks the novels' ambivalence in this area, as Fred Daniels does discover a limit to his desire for unlimited self-assertion. Similar to Raskolnikov, Dmitry, and Ivan, Daniels in a sense goes beyond self-will to find meaning in connection with other people and in recognition of responsibility. In the dialectic of self versus community, *Native Son* and *The Outsider* ultimately side with the individual. "The Man Who Lived Underground," however, shifts the emphasis to the community, or rather it abolishes the dichotomy. For Fred Daniels, much like Shatov and Dmitry, joyously rids himself of his proud isolation and sacrifices himself not out of duty but happiness.

Invisible Man, strongly influenced by "The Man Who Lived Underground" and by Dostoevsky generally, parallels Wright's story as well as *Crime and Punishment, The Devils,* and *The Brothers Karamazov* in its protagonist's growth from the revolt of self-will to the surrender of self-will and to dedication to community. Like the rebellion of Fred Daniels, but unlike that of Cross Damon and Dostoevsky's rebel characters, the Invisible Man's rebellion is not founded consciously on metaphysical or philosophical issues such as his right to do whatever he wishes. Like Daniels, he finds a limit to, or transcends self-will not because he lacks the right to exercise it, but because by gaining new insight into the connectedness of all people he loses his desire to be exclusively self-centered. The radical collectivist "monster" in *Invisible Man*, quite like that in the concurrently published *The Outsider*, exhibits the same sort of bald cynicism and contempt for individual freedom as practiced by Peter Verkhovensky and the Grand Inquisitor. The Invisible Man's eventual acceptance of freedom coupled with responsibility, which is most strongly reminiscent of the

experience of Fred Daniels and Dmitry Karamazov, counterbalances his own
and others' betrayals of humanity.

II

The Devils is similar to *Crime and Punishment* and *The Brothers Karamazov* in that Dostoevsky attempts to demonstrate the power of ineluctable spiritual realities (e.g., the distinction between good and evil, remorse, consciousness of infinity) in the lives of men who have sought consciously to disprove their existence. In *The Devils* Dostoevsky treats materialistic collectivism and revolutionism as outgrowths of individual revolt. As Berdyaev notes, "Dostoevsky studies the results of man's obsession by his own deification under several forms, individual and collective. One consequence is that there is an end to compassion; there is no more mercy" ("Dostoevsky" 576). One of the novel's basic theses holds that the individual's selfish pursuit of freedom as control over others leads directly to despotism. The inhuman system of Shigalyov and Peter Verkhovensky merely codifies the despotic urges of the Underground Man (Jackson, *Underground* 52). Dostoevsky does not concern himself here primarily with attacking political radicalism but with exploring the far more important philosophical and theological beliefs which tend to foster despotism and authoritarianism and which contribute to the stifling of individual personality. In a letter about *The Devils* Dostoevsky wrote, "He who loses his people and nationality, loses the belief of his fathers, and God. Well, if you want to know, this is precisely the theme of my novel" (*Letters* 92). As Berdyaev comments, "Dostoevsky pointed out that the question of socialism was spiritual, not material" (Lowrie 167). As Dostoevsky himself wrote in his *Notebooks for The Possessed*, "Socialism has been embraced not only by those who are hungry, but also by those who are thirsting for a spiritual life'' (201).

The young generation in *The Devils*--Stavrogin, Shatov, Kirilov, and Peter Verkhovensky--are both victims of and rebels against Mr. Verkhovensky's superfluous generation of the 1840s. Those Russians who came of age in the forties dedicated themselves to philosophical idealism and the ultimate worth of the individual soul. Although Dostoevsky often lampooned the egotistical romanticism and naive ineffectuality of much of this generation, and nowhere with more comedy and force than in his portrait of Mr. Verkhovensky, he always retained personal affection for and commitment to their exaltation of the individual and their values of fraternity and compassion. Dostoevsky was one among many Russian writers of the nineteenth century who grappled with the failure of the superfluous men to deliver on their great promise and to accomplish any achievements worthy of their ideals and aspirations. The so-called nihilists of the early sixties retained some of the idealism of their forbears but had been hardened by their fathers' failures in the practical world. Raskolnikov, a rational nihilist, somehow retains his compassion and his sense of honor and decency even as he plans and carries out his murder, the fruit of his desperate desire to *do* something. The influx of materialistic social theories into Russia in the sixties still promoted the vision of earthly harmony, but they based that harmony not on love for one's brothers but on "enlightened self-interest" and "rational advantage." The contradiction in such an idealistic nihilism began to be resolved by the late sixties as it evolved into an incendiary and often violent revolutionism based on an avowed amoralism and a positive hostility to metaphysical considerations while still seeking the improvement of society. The young generation in *The Devils*, which is set in the early 1870s, represents those men who have completed the nihilists' rejection of the superfluous man.

In spite of the nihilists' and revolutionaries' intentions of usefulness, Dostoevsky finds them more tragically wasted than the superfluous men, and yet paradoxically closer to fruition and faith because of the intensity of their negation. The generation of the forties produced many individuals who were lukewarm in their faith or their atheism; Mr. Verkhovensky is an example of an indolent, uncommitted atheistic liberal who never risked or suffered for his freely appropriated and fashionable ideas. The failure of the nihilist-relativist generation to accomplish good is amply suggested in the rain of despair, murder, and suicide which attends Stavrogin, Shatov, Kirilov, and Peter Verkhovensky. But one of Dostoevsky's most central assertions in the novel is that because of this generation's intensity in their investigations of belief and unbelief, even those who proclaim the most extreme form of materialism and atheism (Stavrogin and Kirilov) ultimately come very close to faith. As Tikhon tells Stavrogin, ''The absolute atheist stands on the last rung but one before most absolute faith, while an indifferent man has no faith at all" (679).

Contrary to some critical assessments of *The Devils* as a narrowly political and reactionary statement, it displays a considerable degree of fairness to radicals while it generally subordinates political sympathies to the more significant metaphysical and spiritual analysis of its central characters' states of belief and unbelief. Berdyaev notes the prophetic nature of Dostoevsky's analysis, but he stresses the spiritual focus of the social commentary:

> The Russian revolution has turned out to be a consistent applica-
> tion to life of Russian nihilism, atheism, and materialism--a vast
> experiment based on the denial of all absolute spiritual elements
> in personal and social life.... The bolsheviks are the final Russian
> nihilists.... The Russian revolution has realized what Dostoevsky
> foresaw. (Lowrie 146-47)

Dostoevsky himself wrote a friend while working on the novel, ''What I am writing now is a tendentious thing. I feel like saying everything as passionately as possible. (Let the nihilists and the Westerners scream that I am a reactionary!) To hell with them. I shall say everything to the last word" (Magarshack viii). Yet this was in the early stages of writing the novel, before Dostoevsky discovered how he would develop Shatov, Kirilov, and Stavrogin as individuals struggling with faith. The devils of the title are not necessarily the radicals per se but those who, like Bigger Thomas and Cross Damon, presume to have gone beyond good and evil. Magarshack's claim that Peter Verkhovensky and Stavrogin are only "pegs on which Dostoevsky hung his two most violent dislikes" (xii), namely revolutionaries and the Russian aristocracy, ignores the issue of generational revolt and revenge worked out in Peter as well as the complex psychology and deep spiritual thirst reflected in Stavrogin's project to deny good and evil.

Dostoevsky's fairness to the radicals as human beings capable of compassion and conscience certainly mollifies the novel's occasionally polemical tone. Peter Verkhovensky never shows the least hesitancy or compunction in carrying out his manipulations and murders, but some of his group reflect a basic human decency which recoils from and sometimes regrets such "necessary" measures for eventual social reform. Shatov, impressed with Virginsky and his wife's kindness in helping with the delivery of the baby of Shatov's wife, comments, "So these people possess some generosity after all. A man and his convictions are two different things. Perhaps I haven't been fair to them" (580). Virginsky, who begins to cry out, "It's all wrong!" (601) immediately after the murder of Shatov, further manifests his inner struggle with a subsequent fever and a full confession upon arrest. Shigalyov defects from the group just prior to the murder, not so much because of its immorality but because it contradicts his program for change. And Lyamshin gives the police a full and voluntary account of the plot and the murder, unable to reconcile the goals of radical activity with such debased means.

Dostoevsky surely attempts to make a polemical point with his depiction of Peter Verkhovensky as a nihilistic arch-revolutionary willing to create disorder and to take others' lives without any human feeling. Yet of the novel's revolutionaries and ex-revolutionaries (Shatov, Kirilov, Stavrogin), he is the only one who exhibits an Iago-like glee in evil; of the central characters he alone remains free of disturbing metaphysical questions and struggles with faith.

Dostoevsky carefully distinguishes Peter from socialists and radicals who operate out of deeply felt convictions and a desire to effect ultimately the erection of an improved social order. Several times Peter points out that he is "a rogue and not a Socialist" (421), interested in stirring up trouble and bedlam just for the malicious pleasure of destruction. With Peter, Dostoevsky suggests the backlash or natural retribution which was caused largely by the moral weakness of the superfluous generation. Mr. Verkhovensky's literal abandonment of his son at the age of ten represents his contemporaries' relinquishing of their moral responsibility to fulfill their promises and to act on their grand idealistic talk. The viciousness of Peter's program, then, reflects not so much Dostoevsky's hatred of radicals, as a corollary of his indictment of the superfluous men. Though Peter symbolizes the evil of materialism incarnate, Dostoevsky finds Mr. Verkhovensky more responsible for allowing such a moral vacuum to develop in his own son. In Mr. Verkhovensky's climactic speech before his death, he realizes who are the devils that have plagued Russia, and he sees his own fault: "They are we, we and them, and Peter, and perhaps I at the head of them all, and we shall cast ourselves down, the raving and the possessed, from the cliffs into the sea and shall all be drowned, and serves us right, for that is all we are good for" (648).

Both Peter and Stavrogin are closely related to *Crime and Punishment*'s Svidrigailov and Raskolnikov. Both see themselves as beyond the petty distinctions of good and evil which supposedly apply only to inferior humans. Peter and Stavrogin are guided in their projects of manipulation and outrage mainly by an aesthetic need for diversion, which for Dostoevsky reflects the despair of unbridled self-will (though Stavrogin has the added motive of seeking punishment and self-forgiveness). As suggested above, their completely anti-idealistic amoralism descends directly from their resolution of Raskolnikov's conflict of conscience and self-will. Raskolnikov deludes himself for a long time that the murder and the robbery were done for others; his desire to think of himself as a good man, even while and after committing a murder, eventually forces him to see that he must either confess and surrender or kill himself. Both Peter Verkhovensky and Stavrogin, at least more consistent than Raskolnikov, think of themselves as free of being "good" men. Precisely this singularity of purpose makes these two men chilling figures, again similar in this respect to Svidrigailov. As will be discussed below, however, Stavrogin's exercise of will differs greatly from Peter's in that ultimately he seeks unconsciously to test the limits of his revulsion, in order to recover a sense of good and evil and to obtain forgiveness for a seemingly unforgivable act.

Peter Verkhovensky does not so much embody or adhere to, as much as he exploits the ideology of nihilistic radicalism and socialism for his own selfish purposes of enjoyment and of revenge on his father's generation. He favors Shigalyov's doctrine of establishing despotism and slavery through leveling all human accomplishment and genius to mediocrity. He does not speak as a committed socialist; but Dostoevsky uses his viewpoint to expose what he considers the net effect of a materialistic social organization on the human personality:

> To level the mountains is a good idea, not a ridiculous one. I'm for Shigalyov! We don't want education. . . . The thing we want is obedience. . . . We shall smother every genius in infancy. We shall reduce everything to one common denominator. Full equality. . . . Complete obedience, complete loss of individuality. (419)

Peter stands out as Dostoevsky's statement that such materialistic movements, whether well intentioned or not, ultimately result in the attainment of "one magnificently despotic will" (525), diametrically opposed to individual freedom--the same conclusion Wright reaches in *The Outsider* and Ellison in *Invisible Man*. Peter points toward Dostoevsky's most eloquent realization of this theme in Ivan Karamazov's tale of the Grand Inquisitor.

As the heart of his argument against materialistic collectivism in *The Devils*, Dostoevsky presents the struggles of three men who have rejected materialistic thought and/or collectivist activity and who grope their way consciously or unconsciously toward some type of faith. Each of these men, Shatov, Kirilov, and Stavrogin, has graduated or defected from radical activity, although the latter two still have a nominal commitment to Peter's group. Each is on the way toward some profound metaphysical and mystical or religious awakening; but each remains lost, suspended between two modes of being, right up to his death, which comes as a culmination of his grasping for faith. Shatov has informed Peter and the radical group that he will no longer assist them in any actions; he consciously seeks a restoration of his faith but remains deeply troubled by doubt. His selfless response to his wife's reappearance and to her giving birth to Stavrogin's child imparts to Shatov a joyful faith just before his murder. Kirilov, whose intense materialism has led him paradoxically to a pantheistic mysticism, seeks through suicide either to become a god or to achieve ecstatic union with God. Though he allows the radicals to exploit his suicide for their purposes, Kirilov has no commitment whatever to them. He plans his suicide as the ultimate act of self-will and supposed freedom, but Dostoevsky suggests that Kirilov makes a leap of faith just before taking his own life. Stavrogin's claim that he is beyond good and evil proceeds paradoxically from his deep horror at his responsibility for a young girl's suicide and from his desire for forgiveness. His abandonment of amoralism can be seen in his partly sacrificial suicide, which happens after another particularly heinous act (his allowing the murder of his wife Mary) restores to him the significance of good and evil.

With Shatov Dostoevsky suggests the most strongly the diametrical opposition of materialist-radical groups to individual freedom. Shatov's situation in trying to sunder his ties with Peter's group closely parallels that of Richard Wright attempting to dissociate himself safely from the Communist Party in the early 1940s. When Shatov is warned by Stavrogin that the group may try to kill him, he replies, "I've a right to do that, the right of conscience and thought. . . . I won't put up with it!" (248). Even more than Kirilov or

Stavrogin, Shatov asserts his freedom from the group's control and explains why: "Who are the people I give up? They are enemies of life. . . enemies of individuality and freedom. . . . What is it they have to offer? Envious equality, equality without self-esteem" (575). But like Cross Damon and Fred Daniels, Shatov is made to pay the ultimate price for asserting his freedom.

Before Shatov dies, however, he experiences an existential resolution of his religious doubts. Shatov was deeply influenced by Stavrogin when the latter formerly held religious ideas about true Russians as a "god-bearing people" (253) who are inherently believers in the Orthodox faith. Dostoevsky includes in this discussion, with obvious polemical intention, a corollary of Stavrogin's abandoned creed: that "Socialism is by its very nature bound to be atheistic because it has proclaimed from the very first that it is an atheistic institution and that it intends to organize itself exclusively on the principles of science and reason" (256). Yet, as pointed out above, Dostoevsky knew well from firsthand experience that certain brands of socialism of the thirties and forties were based explicitly on Christian principles and ideals. Here, however, he obscures and denies the once-widespread compatibility of Christianity and socialism, probably because the early sixties had seen the minimization in Russian thought of the idea of free will.

The scandal of Stavrogin's loss of faith and his reckless behavior seriously wounded Shatov's faith because Shatov thus lost his mentor. Shatov's trip with Kirilov to America also implanted doubt in him, presumably because of his separation from Russia. His immediate forgiveness of his wife upon her return and his remarkably warm-hearted acceptance of Stavrogin's son as his own vaults Shatov beyond the doubts and unhappiness that have plagued him for years. He manifests the hallmark for Dostoevsky of depth of spiritual insight: compassion and a joyous understanding of the universality of human responsibility. In a fashion quite similar to the rhapsodic discovery of Dmitry in *The Brothers Karamazov*, Shatov cries out, "We are all to blame, and--if only we were all convinced of that!" (580). Dostoevsky further suggests the profound change in Shatov by the healing of a split between himself and Kirilov and by Shatov's new certainty about God: "He spoke to her of Kirilov, of how they would begin a 'new life,' and 'for ever,' and of the existence of God" (590). Thus Shatov is born also, and his immediate sacrificial death for his wife and her child suggests his spiritual attainment.

Kirilov similarly asserts his independence of despotic group will as he grows in an unconscious faith which belies his materialism and his explicit creed of self-will. Like Stavrogin and Peter Verkhovensky in rejecting morality, Kirilov takes further Raskolnikov's logic that the exceptional individual must dare to kill another, concluding that the only free man is the one who decides to take his own life and who thereby becomes a god. The paradox of Kirilov's past and his career as an architect perfectly summarizes the unusual quality of his negation. This negation dialectically admits of positive action and even a kind of belief--quite unlike the one-sided, destructive negation which Dostoevsky epitomizes in the younger Verkhovensky. The conflict between Kirilov's emerging spiritualism or mysticism based on absolute freedom, and Peter's hardening authoritarianism remains somewhat latent for a while, partly because Kirilov has offered to help the group by claiming responsibility in his suicide note for some of their actions. But when Peter applies pressure on Kirilov regarding the arrangement, Kirilov makes it clear that he is under no obligation to the group and that his cooperation will be purely of his free will. Kirilov walks out in the middle of the meeting at Virginsky's right behind Stavrogin, who has just declared his independence of these people. The freedom-versus-materialism conflict reaches its climax for Kirilov in the dramatic moments before his suicide, when he struggles with Peter and shows signs of abandoning his plan and choosing life over death.

Throughout the novel Dostoevsky depicts Kirilov and Shatov as partaking in a mysterious duality caused by their previous revolutionary-materialistic involvement and by the new understanding each finds before his death. The "double" motif so common in Dostoevsky here suggests that a unified personality has lost its wholeness and suffers until it can achieve reintegration. During their stay in America together, made when both men were under the influence of socialistic ideas, Kirilov and Shatov fell ill, underwent a long convalescence ''on the floor of a hut side by side for four months'' (148), and were cured of strict adherence to those ideas. Both pursued the idea of freedom, but their reflections proved antithetical, Kirilov considering self-will and eventually suicide, and Shatov attempting to return to his Orthodox faith. As Shatov summarizes their divergent approaches to asserting freedom, "He thought of one thing and I of another'' (148). Both understand that their former mentor Stavrogin is thirsting for a spiritual life, yet both are unaware that they too are unconscious believers. They live in the same house but never speak to each other; Shatov's letting Stavrogin in and out of the gate to visit Kirilov further suggests their mysterious bond.

The healing of the rift between the two men coincides with Shatov's open response to his wife's return. Kirilov's avowedly atheistic view symbolizes Shatov's doubt, which disintegrates the closer Kirilov comes to his special brand of mysticism and his intimations of God's existence. When Shatov tells Kirilov of the happiness the latter will find, he is speaking, whether consciously or unconsciously, of the transformation taking place in himself: "Kirilov, if only--if only you'd give up your dreadful delusions and get rid of your atheistic madness--oh, what a man you'd be!'' (567). Dostoevsky further underscores the intimate connection between the two when Shatov's wife concludes that since one has died the other must be dead too: ''They could not find out from her why she should have jumped to the conclusion that her husband, too, had been murdered. She just kept repeating that if Kirilov had been murdered, then, her husband was murdered, because they were together'' (659).

Despite Kirilov's claim that he does not believe in God, he of all these men has the sharpest hunger for a mystical union with God, who he says has tormented him all his life and in whom he more than half believes. Kirilov's statements such as "Life exists, but death doesn't exist at all" (242) and his moments of "eternal harmony" (586) rival the passion of any Christian mystic. He prays often, "to everything," and reads Revelation devoutly with Fedka the convict, indicating an openness to faith. Kirilov is obsessed with the promise of the angel in Revelation that after death there will be no more time. Peter Verkhovensky disdainfully acknowledges that Kirilov really believes in God more than any priest. But Kirilov still suffers from an idolization of his self-will, which he proclaims as the key to his divinization through suicide. For all his growth toward some real belief, Kirilov remains infected in Dostoevsky's view by materialism and rebellion, and for Dostoevsky he represents the connection between the rise of atheism and the prevalence of suicide. Telling Peter that he foresaw the murder of Shatov, Kirilov does, however, acknowledge some responsibility in the matter; and this admission gives further evidence of his nascent belief. Kirilov's momentary rejection of suicide and his struggle with Peter, who threatens to kill him if he does not follow through with the act, reflects a last-minute assertion of life and faith before Kirilov does end his own life.

Stavrogin's rejection of radical collectivism plays a smaller part than Shatov's or Kirilov's, but his development in this respect parallels theirs. His previous dabbling in such activity amounted to only one among his many means of diversion from the crime oppressing his conscience. He has never made a commitment to Peter or his group, but he realizes that his plans to sever all connections with them may result in his murder. Just as Ellison, who never became a member of the Communist Party, knew that he was in some danger for breaking with them, Stavrogin comments to Shatov, "You see, strictly speaking, I don't really belong to the society at all and have never belonged to it, and I am more entitled than you to leave them because I never joined them. . . . And I believe that I, too, have been sentenced" (249). Still he defiantly refuses to answer any of their questions at the crucial meeting at Virginsky's and simply walks out. Stavrogin's general air of independence accounts largely for the lasting impression he has made on Shatov, Kirilov, and even Peter

Verkhovensky, who emulates his hero's unconcern with political causes and exercises self-will to a demonic degree.

Stavrogin lives a life of conscious and outrageous amoralism and self-will which covers up his despair over an "unforgivable" act he committed several years ago, while it also masks his singular desire for forgiveness. His rape of the eleven-year-old Matryosha, and his allowing her to hang herself, comprise his great sin which torments him daily. Immediately after her suicide Stavrogin became, in his words,

> conscious of being a low and despicable coward simply because I was glad of having escaped and that I should never again be an honorable man (neither here, nor after death, nor ever). . . . I formulated for the first time in my life what appeared to be the rule of my life, namely, that I neither know nor feel good or evil, and that I have not only lost any sense of it, but that there is neither good nor evil. (692)

He perversely defies himself to do something which will even compare with this crime and resurrect his sense of shame or responsibility. Thus Stavrogin's project is to test the limits of his own revulsion. Unlike Raskolnikov, who seeks to stifle his moral sense, Stavrogin tries to rediscover his, but only through the dialectical means of this challenge. Ironically, the re-establishment of his moral sense, which becomes a rebirth for him at the end of the novel, also plunges him into deeper despair and then suicide, for he cannot live with his now-accepted responsibility for the death of Matryosha and the murder of his wife. Much as with Svidrigailov and Ivan Karamazov, the birth of a moral sense in Stavrogin, while undoubtedly a healthy spiritual progression, proves risky and in a sense life-threatening, for it clarifies the choices one must make between living with responsibility and dying to avoid it.

Dostoevsky develops the theme of unconscious faith to the greatest degree in Stavrogin. Kirilov states paradoxically yet precisely the quandary of a personality resisting its deeply felt belief: ''If Stavrogin believes in God, then he doesn't believe that he believes. And if he doesn't believe, then he doesn't believe that he doesn't believe" (611). The fact that Stavrogin's only purpose, as he says, is to forgive himself indicates that he has never fully abandoned his ideas of right and wrong. His marriage to Mary Lebyatkin, described by Shatov as proceeding from his "passion for remorse" (261), was part of his conscious intention to seek "boundless suffering" (702). Stavrogin's self-punishment includes his daily summoning up the horrible image of the dead Matryosha shaking her fist at him. Dostoevsky, in parallel fashion to his development of Ivan's regeneration, shows Stavrogin balking at a positive expression of belief but approaching it nonetheless through intimations of the devil, as he asks Tikhon, "But can one believe in the devil without believing in God?" (678). Tikhon finds Stavrogin to be one of those "absolute atheists" (679) who stand just short of absolute faith; in fact, based on Stavrogin's belief in expiatory suffering, Tikhon concludes that he already believes "in everything already" (703). The monk sees, however, that Stavrogin's decision to accept more suffering by announcing his marriage and publishing his confession involves a terrible temptation to commit some new and greater crime in order to avoid the humiliation. Despite Stavrogin's statement that he does not want to kill any more people, even his wife Mary suspects the danger he presents to her. He clearly condones Fedka's murder of Mary and her brother, which allows Stavrogin to run off with the engaged Lisa Drozdov, who also loses her life because of her connection with him. Stavrogin says in his letter just before his suicide that he recognizes his personal guilt and responsibility for the deaths of Mary and Lisa; this admission indicates that he can no longer take refuge in his amoralism, and it suggests a virtual conversion and the completion of his process of becoming aware that he *does* believe. He kills himself because he cannot bear, or chooses not bear, the memory of Matryosha together with the new guilt for the other deaths. In a sense his project of defying himself ever again to feel the legitimacy of good or evil succeeds--yet at great cost to Mary and Lisa and to Stavrogin himself.

Although *The Devils* features a bleak array of treachery, infidelity, mental breakdowns, murders, and suicides, the novel's implications for both personal and national growth beyond materialism remain optimistic. Each of the three main characters, although caught for most of the novel in his struggle between materialistic collectivism and religious belief, finds a highly particularized though qualified kind of deliverance by the time of his death. The sacrifice of each man's life (Shatov's for his wife and her baby; Kirilov's for Shatov's new belief; Stavrogin's for Dasha Shatov, to save her from a life with him in exile) constitutes the essential leap of faith and signifies a victory of the spirit. Thus Dostoevsky sees great hope in the doubts and even in the negation of such a troubled generation. In *The Devils* Dostoevsky prophesies with chilling accuracy the cataclysm of the Russian revolution. But he also implies possible regeneration in the idea that absolute negation leads either to suicide or to eventual conversion.

III

In *The Brothers Karamazov* Dostoevsky focuses his polemic not on radicalism or anarchism, which had abated somewhat by the late 1870s when he wrote it, but rather on atheism and materialistic collectivism as the primary enemies of freedom in the modern era. He intended his last novel as an expose of atheism which would show the dire consequences of its consistent and seemingly humane application to human problems. Although Dostoevsky grants some concessions to socialism, and especially to Christian socialism (which he refused to recognize in *The Devils*), essentially he hardens his position against it. Again, as in *Crime and Punishment* and *The Devils*, he presents a man, Ivan, testing out a materialistic idea which reflects self-will, suffering for his denial of transcendence, and eventually achieving some spiritual understanding precisely because of the failure of that idea. As in *Crime*

150

and Punishment, Dostoevsky analyzes the meaning of taking one apparently useless life and the consequences of trying to deny the responsibility for that act. Again he asserts the sacred value of human life and condemns any utilitarian or mathematical attempt to condone murder by offsetting it with a multitude of rationally determined advantages. But whereas in *Crime and Punishment* Dostoevsky concentrates on the guilt only of the actual murderer, in *The Brothers Karamazov* he asserts the responsibility of seemingly uninvolved and innocent individuals, namely Alyosha, Dmitry, and Ivan. The novel's central thesis that all men are responsible for all others issues, however, not in gloom or a weighty sense of duty for the main characters, but in a paradoxical feeling of joy and freedom. Indeed, Dostoevsky argues that individual freedom, which is antithetical to atheistic collectivism, is the necessary condition for personal growth and the source of personal dignity.

The Brothers Karamazov develops in a similar manner to *The Devils* in showing three young men who must die in a symbolic sense in order to resolve their doubts and tensions and to start living. In *The Devils*, where none of the main characters survives, Dostoevsky concentrates more on the despair and darkness attending various kinds of doubt and rebellion. *The Brothers Karamazov*, on the other hand, offers much more light. For although each of the three brothers must go metaphorically underground, each also rises to new life. Each needs to revolt in pursuit of self-will in order to transcend or surrender self-will and to choose an identity of deeper compassion. Alyosha loses his dependence on his religious mentor and his very monastic vocation on the way to discovering his calling of service in the world. Dmitry is purged of his reckless passion through his explicit acceptance of moral responsibility for the murder he does not commit. Ivan undergoes the most profound and complete transformation, forced to surrender his rationalistic denial of God and morality by his growing sense of complicity in the murder of his father. *The Brothers Karamazov* succeeds in its artistic representation of classic Christian themes because of the complexity, variety, and individualization of the struggles of these men toward a higher spiritual plane Dostoevsky's last novel excels in its promulgation of the positive ideal of service to humanity not merely in the words of Father Zosima but in these characters' painful and credible meanderings through forms of negation.

While Dostoevsky in *The Brothers Karamazov* qualifies his criticisms of his ideological opponents, he attacks them more directly and more explicitly than in *The Devils*. Whereas in the earlier novel he argues that socialism and Christianity are irreconcilable, here he admits what he knew from personal experience in the 1840s, that they can be compatible. Dostoevsky implies respect for this combination of beliefs in the words of a superintendent of detectives: "There are a few peculiar men who believe in God and are Christians, but at the same time are socialists. Those are the people we are most afraid of. They are dreadful people! The socialist who is a Christian is more to be dreaded than a socialist who is an atheist" (679). In a similar spirit, Zosima exhorts his fellow monks not to hate "the atheists, the teachers of evil, the materialists" (149) because many among them are good people. Yet Dostoevsky clearly disapproves of the majority of socialistic activity as "the tower of Babel built without God, not to mount Heaven from earth but to set up Heaven on earth" (20). In letters written before and during the composition of the novel, Dostoevsky insists on the deadening effect of socialism and the cynicism of many socialists:

> Contemporary socialism in Europe, and here, constantly dismisses Christ, and concerns itself first of all with *bread*, calls upon science and maintains that the only reasons for all man's miseries are *poverty*, the struggle for survival, "the environment ruined him." . . . But suppose you gave them Beauty and Bread at the same time? Then you would deprive man of *work*, *individuality*, *self-sacrifice*, and *the sacrifice of one's goods for one's neighbor*; in short, all life, the ideal of life would be taken away. . . . Bread, the tower of Babel, and the total enslavement of the freedom of conscience--that is what the desperate nay-sayer and atheist comes to. The difference lies in that our socialists (and you know

very well that it is not merely the underground nihilists) are conscious Jesuits and liars who do not admit that their ideal is the ideal of coercing human consciousness and reducing humanity to a herd of cattle, while my socialist (Ivan Karamazov) is a sincere man who admits openly that he agrees with the Grand Inquisitor's view of humanity and that Christ's faith (seemingly) raised man much higher than he in fact is. (754, 759)

Instead of revolutionary radicals per se Dostoevsky pursues those he considers ideological radicals such as Ivan and Rakitin, whose atheistic theories he sees as undermining society itself. Although Dostoevsky thinks Ivan to be in error, he maintains respect for him because Ivan's atheism, like Cross Damon's but unlike Rakitin's, brings him not smugness or ease but grief and puzzlement. Dostoevsky offers a more pointed critique, however, of shallow atheists, liberals, and supposed humanitarians such as Rakitin and Madame Khokhlakov, who philosophize grandly about universal love but find themselves unable to love actual, individual people. As Dostoevsky comments, "Ivan Fyodorovich is profound; he isn't one of the contemporary atheists who merely show the narrowness of their world-view and the dullness of their dull little capacities in their disbelief" ("Notebooks" 769). The novel demonstrates how materialistic ideas filter down from master (Ivan) to servant (Smerdyakov) and even affect the young generation in Kolya, who proudly proclaims he is a socialist and whose several destructive ventures parody Smerdyakov's murder of Fyodor Karamazov. Through Dmitry's remarks Dostoevsky scorns the deterministic viewpoint exemplified in the morally degenerate Rakitin, who interprets Dmitry's apparent murder of his father as a direct effect of environment. Dostoevsky treats Rakitin much more harshly than he does any character in *The Devils*, showing him as cynical, glib, and greedy: the unheroic brand of unbeliever, in contrast to Ivan.

With the story of the Grand Inquisitor, which is a by-product of Ivan's earnest struggle with the mystery of suffering and the burden of freedom, Dostoevsky epitomizes the rationale of materialistic collectivism, a rationale echoed in the attitudes of Gil and Hilton in *The Outsider* and Jack and the Brotherhood in *Invisible Man*. Ivan endorses a collectivism which levels society and eliminates freedom in exchange for perfect control of human passions and the end of all vice and crime. He finds absolutely unacceptable a world in which the terrible burden of freedom often results in persecution and the suffering of innocent people. Therefore Ivan rejects and indicts Christ for calling men to exercise their freedom and thus to risk failure and moral retrogression. Robert Jackson points out that Ivan, the thoughtful and humane atheist, at least faces the problem of suffering squarely: "Both the antirationalist Underground Man and the rationalist Ivan arrive at the same conclusion-- the conclusion of uncompromising idealists--namely, that a harmony which does not cope with the problem of suffering, the problem of the irrational, is unacceptable" (*Underground* 53). D. H. Lawrence misinterprets the ideological and artistic intent of the story of the Grand Inquisitor and of the whole novel, claiming that Dostoevsky agrees with Ivan and the Inquisitor that Christ is inadequate and that freedom is too great a burden for man (830). Dostoevsky indicates that he is aware of the eloquence of the Inquisitor's argument but that the entire novel opposes that view: "Those blockheads have never even conceived so powerful a rejection of God as exists in the Inquisitor and the preceding chapter, to which *the whole book* will serve as answer" ("Notebooks" 769). In a letter Dostoevsky comments further on his intent with the Grand Inquisitor:

> Its meaning, as you will see from the text I sent, is the depiction of extreme blasphemy and the kernel of the idea of destruction of our time, in Russia, among our youth who have broken away from reality, and together with the blasphemy and anarchy, their refutation in the last words of the Elder Zosima. ("Letters" 757)

The refutation of the Grand Inquisitor only begins, in abstract form, with Zosima's life story and spiritual exhortations, and reaches fulfillment in the remainder of the novel's concrete, existential applications in the lives of the three brothers. Still the words of Zosima themselves, which Dostoevsky once referred to as "the culminating point of the novel" ("Letters" 760), are both simple and profound in their estimation of the destructive individualism which Dostoevsky finds at the heart of atheistic socialism, and which he says makes impossible any true solidarity:

> To transform the world, to recreate if afresh, men must turn into another path psychologically. Until you have become really, in actual fact, a brother to everyone, brotherhood will not come to pass. No sort of scientific teaching, no kind of common interest, will ever teach men to share property and privileges with equal consideration for all. . . . The true security is to be found in social solidarity rather than in isolated individual effort. But this individualism must inevitably have an end, and all will suddenly understand how unnaturally they are separated from one another. (282, 283)

Zosima's stories about his brother, his duel, and the mysterious stranger illustrate the primacy of spiritual consciousness over material comfort. The rest of the novel features several incidents which support this theme through individuals' free abandonment of their "rational advantage" for expressions of personality and dignity (e.g., Snegiryov's trampling on the money Alyosha offers him, and Ivan's testimony against himself at Dmitry's trial and thereby risking madness).

Through Zosima and Alyosha, Dostoevsky proposes the practical ideal of active love and the service of humanity as the best hope for personal fulfillment and social betterment. But an individual's realization of the happiness to which he is born must be preceded by a death-and-birth cycle of surrender of self-will and a new knowledge of intimate connectedness with all others. This regeneration becomes not an abstract or intellectual, but a heartfelt personal responsibility to live for others. A prominent corollary of Dostoevsky's thesis holds that the individual who acts courageously and lovingly often will be regarded as insane. But as Zosima insists, "a man must set an example, and so draw men's souls out of their solitude, and spur them to some act of brotherly love, even if he seems crazy, so that the great idea may not die" (283).

Alyosha's experience of doubt, rebellion, and new faith presents Dostoevsky's first major response to the Grand Inquisitor. The most spiritually advanced of the Karamazov brothers, Alyosha already has dedicated his life to the service of humanity through his monastic vocation. But his faith lacks maturity and solidity, for he places too much significance on external details surrounding the death of his beloved mentor Zosima. When Alyosha's expected miracle does not occur, he rebels by leaving the monastery, breaking his fast, and nearly beginning an affair with Grushenka. Alyosha becomes a more credible and in a sense a more likable character when he doubts his faith and engages in the Karamazov revolt of sensuality. Grushenka restores his faith by a simple act of compassion when she learns that he is mourning his spiritual father. Alyosha's rebirth climaxes in his vision of a joyous Zosima calling him to celebrate Christ's presence in the world. Afterward Alyosha becomes aware that he is partially responsible for his father's death because during his rebellion he neglected to contact Dmitry and help him through his crisis of passion. Alyosha finds his new calling in a life of more direct service to others outside the monastery. Even the holy Alyosha profits spiritually from succumbing to the temptation of self-will and struggling to a difficult new level of freedom.

The second answer to the Inquisitor comes when Dmitry overcomes the powerful forces of passion and anger drawing him toward the murder of his father, demonstrating that even the most dissolute men are capable of freely chosen restraint. At the center of the novel's action, the dynamic Dmitry seeks and accepts regeneration much more explicitly than either Alyosha or Ivan. Like Rogozhin of *The Idiot*, Dmitry is all but consumed by passion which threatens to spill over into violence, and he risks the utmost degradation (the loss of his honor, and the murder of his father) to satisfy his desire. His whole life is a revolt against moderation and a debauch of self-assertion. But his openness to a radical spiritual transformation prepares Dmitry to resist murder at the last minute and to experience the sudden, unexpected metamorphosis of his passion for Grushenka into love. Unlike the revolt of Alyosha and Ivan, Dmitry's self-assertion does not involve metaphysical or religious rebellion but simple, selfish desire. He never abandons, suspends, or questions his belief in God, and his expectations of a miracle in his life strengthen him to receive divine grace and to resist the urge when he might have killed his father. Dmitry holds tenaciously to his wish for honor even when he feels he has lost it by spending the rest of the 3,000 roubles of Katerina Ivanovna.

While brother Ivan labors to argue away his moral sense, Dmitry struggles to retain his, in spite of the beatings he administers to Snegiryov and his father, the shame he causes his fiancee by chasing other women, and the scandal of his drunken revelries. He knows and accepts the categories of good and evil which Ivan thinks he has overcome. Dmitry thinks of his horrible actions as shames and sins; he feels that his fidelity at least to the Christian world-view provides him with grace when he nearly kills his father: ''God was watching over me'' (370). His dream of the "poor babe," parallel to Alyosha's dream of Cana of Galilee (and echoed in "The Man Who Lived Underground" with Daniels's dream of the drowning baby), imparts to Dmitry an ecstatic vision of the interconnectedness of human suffering and of his role in alleviating some of that suffering. Although he does not kill his father, he accepts culpability because he meant to kill him and because he sees his suffering as helping others: "It's for the babes I'm going. Because we are all responsible for all. For all the babes. I go for all, because someone must go for all. I didn't kill father, but I've got to go. I accept it" (560). Dmitry's probable escape to America does not diminish his embracing a life "underground" because his life there will be a painful exile in a land he regards as hopelessly materialistic and unspiritual. The paradoxical rhapsody of his proclamation of responsibility, together with his surrender of self-assertion for the sake of the community, is duplicated by Wright and Ellison in the awakenings of Fred Daniels and the Invisible Man.

Dostoevsky completes his refutation of the Grand Inquisitor with Ivan's surrender of rationalistic amoralism when he reluctantly acknowledges his guilt for Fyodor Karamazov's murder. Though not as externally dramatic as Dmitry's predicament, the conflict of Ivan, whom D. H. Lawrence aptly calls "the greatest of the three brothers, pivotal" (830), becomes the most life-threatening and therefore receives the climactic position of most importance. While Raskolnikov's rationalistic theory claims the right of superior individuals to take life at will, Ivan's theory goes much further, deducing from atheism the justification of all crime, including murder, for anyone. Both Raskolnikov and Ivan emerge from their excessive isolation from humanity ironically, in that their seemingly humane concerns result in murder. Their theories result in at least some involvement with other people, which proves crucial to their development: Raskolnikov with Sonya and her family, and Ivan with Smerdyakov and his brothers. Though both Stavrogin and Ivan deny the existence of good and evil, and similarly condone murders and later recognize responsibility for them, Stavrogin posits his theory out of revulsion for his earlier crime, while Ivan argues his theory from reason. Stavrogin asserts amorality as a reaction to his internalized but repressed horror at what he has done; Ivan asserts amorality as a purely rational proposition, the failure of which results directly in a similar sense of horror. Ivan refuses to believe in a God who would allow such great suffering in the world, especially the suffering of innocent children, who in no way can be said to have transgressed or sinned. Yet Ivan's conscious and compassionate humanism, combined with rationalism which recognizes no virtue, results in the profoundly ironic end of compassion, in the justification of and tendency toward murder. Cross Damon lacks Ivan's sensitive concern for innocent suffering; but he shares with Ivan an acceptance of "ultimate" freedom in a godless universe, and finds himself similarly able to justify any action. Cross, however, never comes to a recognition that he lacks the right to kill whomever he wishes.

Ivan gradually becomes aware that he has desired and indirectly caused his father's death, and this irresistible knowledge leads him eventually to nullify his theory by admitting his moral guilt. The central moral act of the novel parallels that of *The Devils*: just as Stavrogin effectively causes his wife Mary's death by giving Fedka tacit permission to murder her, Ivan leaves his father's house expecting and counting on his father's murder either by Smerdyakov or Dmitry. Ivan deludes himself that he has washed his hands of the matter, but even as he rides the train for Moscow he stays up all night and finally whispers to himself, "I am a scoundrel" (260). He keeps the full implications of his action, however, hidden from himself until nearly the end of the novel. With great artistry and subtlety Dostoevsky develops in Book Eleven Ivan's moral awakening. Ivan's worsening nervous debility and illness reflects the crisis of his theory, which is tested and refuted, not through rational argument but through the pain of the discovery of conscience. Over the course of Ivan's three visits to Smerdyakov, he both seeks and hides from the truth of his complicity and guilt. Once Ivan admits to himself that if Smerdyakov killed Fyodor Pavlovich, then Ivan himself is guilty, he approaches full understanding of the situation.

But Ivan's theory of amoralism proves very difficult for him to jettison, and he closes his mind to the evident likelihood that Smerdyakov is the killer. In the first two interviews Smerdyakov provides ample and clear hints that he has been Ivan's instrument, but Ivan resists recognition. Smerdyakov's illness, a barometer of his own guilt and need to force the truth on Ivan, grows worse as he fails for a while to make Ivan see. When Smerdyakov finally admits outright that he killed Fyodor Pavlovich, Ivan can no longer evade the massive correction required to his theory and his life. Smerdyakov, the student now become the teacher, astutely sums up the metaphysical balance sheet:

> You are still responsible for it all, since you knew of the murder, sir, and charged me to do it, sir, and went away knowing all about it. And so I want to prove to your face this evening that you are the only real murderer in the whole affair, and I am not the real murderer, though I did kill him. You are the rightful murderer. (594)

Dostoevsky suggests a duality between Ivan and Smerdyakov; the latter's suicide and symbolic internalization in Ivan represent Ivan's decisive recognition of evil within.

Despite Smerdyakov's taunt (echoing the Grand Inquisitor) that Ivan will prefer the safety and comfort of silence over the humiliating and probably useless testimony against himself at the trial, Ivan does follow through, sacrificing his theory and virtually admitting that a restored belief in virtue opens the possibility of belief in God. Ivan rescues the frozen peasant whom he knocked to the ground and left for dead on the way to his last interview with Smerdyakov; with his decision to testify against himself he has suddenly acquired real compassion and the ethic of social responsibility. This actual peasant has the same symbolic significance for Ivan as the visionary "babe" does for Dmitry, and the drowning baby for Fred Daniels: both are embodiments of suffering humanity. Ivan's conversation with his imagined or real devil serves the same function in his spiritual development as Stavrogin's talks with a devil: the creeping intimation that a negative spiritual universe implies a positive one, that belief in a devil entails belief in God. Ivan finds his incipient faith expressed, ironically and mockingly, by his devil, in words that echo those of Stavrogin: "Does proving there's a devil prove that there's a God?" (603). Ivan nearly loses his mind during this torturous cross-examination by a devil who may be only a side-effect of his brain fever, but whose insight into such men as Ivan, Kirilov, and Stavrogin is remarkable: "They can contemplate such depths of belief and disbelief at the same moment that sometimes it really seems that they are within a hairsbreadth of being 'turned upside down'" (613).

Ivan's proclamation of his guilt at Dmitry's trial involves a high degree of personal risk, but his appearance saves Ivan from probable madness and initiates his new life. He sees clearly that performing this virtuous act negates his idea that God and virtue do not exist. He also understands that his very life is threatened by this shock to his psyche. But a failure or refusal to testify would have destroyed Ivan, for it would have kept him in a state of unbearable conflict.

160

Dostoevsky ridicules the worldly point of view exhibited at the trial, that Ivan is a madman, reinforcing the theme that the courageous and heroic act of love is often regarded as insanity. Ivan vacillates between confession and silence even as he begins to testify, but he decides to end his isolation, to accept suffering, and to go underground in the same sense as Dmitry. After testifying, Ivan, whom Katerina calls "that hero of honor and conscience" who "has sacrificed himself for his brother" (717), becomes very ill with a high fever, reflecting his lack of final resolution. As in the depiction of Raskolnikov in his early days in Siberia, and of Kirilov and Stavrogin before their deaths, Dostoevsky refrains from representing a simplistic conversion, showing instead a complex and proud personality which has not quite acquired a spiritual view. Both Dmitry and Alyosha believe that Ivan is superior to them and that he will recover. When he emerges from his underground and attains unity of action and thought, Ivan also will realize new purpose and strength.

Dostoevsky's response to the Grand Inquisitor does not exist merely at a level of preachments or abstract theology, but becomes fully embodied in the vital, passionate strivings of Alyosha, Dmitry, and Ivan Karamazov, in each of whom the positive ideal of love and universal responsibility is born. *The Brothers Karamazov* thus offers much more hope for the future than either *Crime and Punishment* or *The Devils*. The community of boys united by Ilyusha's suffering and death represents Russia's turning away from the artificial socialist anthill to true solidarity based on respect for the individual.

IV

"The Man Who Lived Underground" attains a higher degree of ideological and artistic unity than *Native Son* or *The Outsider*, for it treats revolt more consistently as a stage of development and does not justify or mitigate its offenses against community. This story influenced *Invisible Man* with its powerful blend of realism and symbolism and its basic situation of a protagonist who brackets the world by retreating underground. Wright had quit the Communist Party in 1942, two years before publishing this story, and his concentration here on individual experience and truth implies his disinterest in collectivism. Margolies notes that with this story Wright achieves a new universality beyond the bounds of protest literature:

> Heretofore dread, terror, and guilt had been the lot of the Negro in a world that had thrust upon him the role of a despised inferior. Now they are the attributes of all mankind. . . . Now these standards are held to be as illusory for whites as they had always been inaccessible for Negroes. When Fred Daniels attempts to educate men to this truth, he is shot and killed. (79)

This story clearly resolves *Native Son*'s ambivalence on naturalism and self-will, asserting instead existential freedom coupled with social responsibility. Of all of Wright's works, one finds the influence of Dostoevsky the strongest here. Wright again argues man's need to free himself from oppressive circumstances and extorted promises. But Wright adopts Dostoevsky's theme of personal accountability even in the apparently innocent person as the key to the transcendence of self-will and to true freedom. After a while Fred Daniels finds his nearly absolute freedom underground to be meaningless and absurd. When he begins to feel responsible for the suicide he could have prevented, he parts company with Bigger Thomas and Cross Damon, who in their rebellion deny responsibility for killings they cause directly.

Fred Daniels, innocent of murder but pursued by the police, who have extracted a false confession from him, undergoes a psychic journey into himself and into the souls of all men, learning of his own guilt and that of all humanity. He encounters a number of scenes representing the alienation and suffering not just of black people but of all people. Daniels feels pity and anger for the black congregation he observes because he thinks they will never get the peace or happiness for which they pray. The dead baby floating in the sewer arouses in him a similar feeling of nothingness and a vision which he cannot eradicate from his mind. Exploring metaphorical lower depths, he reflects on the dead bodies in the undertaker's, the coalbin and furnace, and the movie audience, which he sees as a nadir of lifelessness and a mockery of life. Daniels rejects the moral corruption and materialism in the aboveground world of "obscene sunshine" (550), the "wild forest filled with death" (549), as he gathers the symbols of that materialism, namely money, diamonds, and jewelry, in a mocking celebration of their uselessness to him below. Amid this freedom from the tyranny of material objects, Daniels recalls his name only with difficulty, for he has left behind the false identity forced on him by the other world; his "death" logically must precede his rising to a freely chosen identity and to a sharing of his new knowledge with others. He accepts his novice status as he pecks away at a typewriter and begins the movement toward a new world and a new self.

Daniels initially regards himself as innocent not just of the murder of which he has been accused, but of any harmful proclivities or desires. By stressing Daniels's initial concern with his innocence, Wright aligns him with the congregation, who Daniels thinks "should stand up unrepentant" (523) because they are innocent as well. Thus the tone of the first part of the story resembles the dominant attitude of defiant innocence in *Native Son* and *The Outsider*. As Daniels changes, however, the tone of innocence is surrendered, in clear contrast to the novels. At first Daniels feels there is nothing wrong with taking the money or the diamonds because morally speaking he does not steal them but merely picks them up, not for any value to himself but ironically for their misplaced value to the "dead" people above. Neither does he feel bad about taking other objects such as the radio, the meat cleaver, and the tools, because he feels, as do Bigger and Cross, that all everyday morality has been suspended for him in these extraordinary circumstances. Yet he does not even approach the extremes of amorality and violence of Bigger and Cross. In spite of his conscious assertions of innocence, Daniels experiences the feeling of guilt several times without being able to account for it rationally: "They know I didn't do anything, he muttered. Though innocent, he felt guilty, condemned" (538). Daniels's ingrained guilt resembles both Cross's guilt infused by his mother and Bigger's dread forced on him by the hostile environment. Wright does not attempt to explain the origin or the reason for this feeling, but he suggests that its hold on the human personality and the unconscious mind is unshakable:

> Why was this sense of guilt so seemingly innate, so easy to come by, to think, to feel, so verily physical? It seemed that when one felt this guilt one was retracing in one's feelings a faint pattern designed long before; it seemed that one was always trying to remember a gigantic shock that had left a haunting impression upon one's body which one could not forget or shake off, but which had been forgotten by the conscious mind, creating in one's life a state of eternal anxiety. (555)

Daniels at first does not regret being the cause of the false accusations against the boy and the watchman, thinking that each at least will become aware of the universal injustice of life, of the "secret of his existence, the guilt that he could never get rid of" (555). At this point Daniels sees no reason for this primordial sense of guilt, yet he asserts that even the innocent watchman has always shared it.

As long as Daniels rejects his own personal responsibility for the world, he sees himself as totally free because he is alone and not connected to or committed to anyone. Believing in this void-like version of freedom, he endorses a moral relativism much like that of Stavrogin and Ivan Karamazov, as well as Bigger and Cross, according to which, "Maybe *any*thing's right, he mumbled. Yes, if the world as men had made it was right then anything else was right, any act a man took to satisfy himself, murder, theft, torture" (551). By the end of the story, however, Daniels finds that this apparent freedom is as absurd as having diamonds in a sewer. Wright weaves prefigurements of Daniels's eventual transformation throughout the story. Try as he may, Daniels cannot shake the image of the dead baby or its symbolic import as a representative of human suffering. In his dream he attempts to save the drowning woman and the baby, but he fails when his faith gives out and he can no longer stand upon the water. This dream operates for Wright the same way Dmitry's dream of the babe does in *The Brothers Karamazov*, indicating the birth of an intense sense of compassion concomitant with a discovery of responsibility. Daniels's pity for the man stealing money from the safe, and his desire to help the metaphorically dead people in the theater, also foreshadow this change.

Daniels's realization of his personal responsibility for the suicide of the watchman parallels each Karamazov brother's discovery that he is responsible for a murder he did not actually commit. This discovery fires him with the wish to begin a new life of sharing with others his knowledge of universal accountability. Even before his personal awakening, Daniels feels a strong irrational impulse to act while he also has presentiments of the enormous risk which an emergence from underground would involve. He dreams of rising aboveground and confronting the police, and then of watching his own nude body on a table, subconsciously aware that he will pay with his life for his free actions. The watchman's suicide in front of his eyes, which was occasioned by Daniels's theft and which he easily could have prevented, jolts him into a direct awareness of his responsibility and an immediate decision to go aboveground. As with Ivan Karamazov, Daniels's acceptance of suffering spells the end of his amoralism and of selfish, rootless freedom. His self-will has been emptied of meaning. As with Dmitry Karamazov, who accepts the torture of exile and nominal freedom in America, Daniels's acceptance of moral guilt brings not sorrow or regret but release and joy, as his actions are "informed with precision, his muscular system reinforced from a reservoir of energy" (559). Like Dmitry, Daniels has found the freedom of acting for others less burdensome than that of acting for himself.

Daniels confronts some severe ironies and rejections as he begins his new life of uncertain but dedicated prophesy. As he struggles to give words to his insight, the church congregation does not listen to him, regarding him as drunk or insane, much as the people in court treat Ivan. To the police Daniels's appearance becomes an embarrassment, for they have the real killer after having beaten a signed confession from Daniels. Wright offers a variation on the scene where Raskolnikov surrenders awkwardly at the police station. In *Crime and Punishment* Raskolnikov admits his legal guilt but feels no moral compunction for his murders; here, Daniels is not concerned any longer with claiming legal innocence, which he now regards as incidental, but with proclaiming his basic guilt toward all his brothers and the responsibility of all men for each other: "They said I killed her. But it doesn't make any difference. I'm guilty. . . . All the people I saw was guilty" (565). The aboveground world now takes on an aura of unreality for him, since it unnaturally refuses to accept his knowledge and his sacrifice. The police destroy his confession; society rejects his prophetic word with all its potential for healing.

Despite the harshness of the story's conclusion with Daniels's murder in the sewer, Wright emphasizes the ecstasy and complete transformation of Daniels toward selflessness, fellowship, and compassion, which, he implies, transcend and ultimately defeat cynicism and hatred. Whereas Alyosha, Dmitry, and Ivan Karamazov go metaphorically underground to accept their responsibility and suffering, Daniels decides to rise to the corrupt everyday world to do the same because that world is ironically dark and threatening.

"The Man Who Lived Underground" connects with *The Brothers Karamazov* also in the theme that some people must sacrifice themselves so that "the great idea" of which Dostoevsky speaks may not die, that the ideal of a community of love may survive. Indeed, Dostoevsky's biblical epigraph for his last novel, that the corn of wheat must die in order to bear fruit, applies as well to Wright's story. Daniels feels great joy because he has come to love people through observing their suffering. He passionately desires that through sharing his experience underground "soon everybody would be governed by the same impulse of pity" (574). The tone of the final pages approaches the bliss Dmitry experiences when he dedicates himself to the service of others, even underground. Dmitry says,

> Oh yes, we shall be in chains and there will be no freedom, but then, in our great sorrow, we shall rise again to joy, without which man cannot live nor God exist, for God gives joy: it's His privilege--a grand one. . . . One cannot exist prison without God; it's even more impossible than out of prison. And then we men underground will sing from the bowels of the earth a tragic hymn to God with Whom is joy. Hail to God and His joy! (650)

Fred Daniels shares Dmitry's ecstasy:

> They did not believe him now, but they would. A mood of high selflessness throbbed in him. He could barely contain his rising spirits. They would see what he had seen; they would feel what he had felt. . . . He wanted to make a hymn, prance about in physical ecstasy, throw his arm about the policemen in fellowship. (573)

The brutal murder of Daniels stands as a statement of the ultimate cost of fellowship and as the epitome of that high selflessness. Thus Wright intends this death to be understood as a fruitful sacrifice which should not depress but uplift, for such acts help men to come out of their solitude and eventually to reconstruct the community.

V

Similar to all the protagonists discussed in Dostoevsky's and Wright's work, the Invisible Man also experiences man's need for revolt in the effort to discover freedom and identity. The Invisible Man rebels against his manipulation by others and asserts what he regards as his freedom. But he becomes a slave of self-will, which blinds him to his self-deception and further exploitation by others. Like the revolt of Dmitry and Fred Daniels, his is non-metaphysical and non-intellectual, and is therefore in a sense more universal than Ivan's or Cross's. The Invisible Man does not consciously conclude that he is beyond good and evil, nor does he pursue a nihilistic experiment; rather, he feels and lives out man's urge for total freedom without considering the cost to others. Freedom beckons him throughout the novel, but he tends to settle for a relatively shallow, selfish version which offers him greater power. He begins to sense the burden of freedom when he accepts social responsibility, but he also learns of freedom's lightness and creativity in possibility.

Similar to Dostoevsky and Wright (especially in "The Man Who Lived Underground"), Ellison in *Invisible Man* opposes philosophical materialism, collectivism, and naturalism with his protagonist's evolving awareness of responsibility and his deepening sense of virtually limitless freedom. As noted above, Ellison studied Dostoevsky's craft very closely, especially that of *The Brothers Karamazov*. Among the influences on *Invisible Man*, one of the clearest is *Notes from Underground*, whose first, confessional sentence, "I'm a sick man . . . a mean man" (90), finds an echo in Ellison's opening: "I am an invisible man" (3). In his introduction to the thirtieth anniversary edition of the novel Ellison says of his narrator, "Having nothing to lose, and by way of providing myself the widest field for success or failure, I associated him, ever so distantly, with the narrator of Dostoevsky's *Notes from Underground*, and with that I began to structure the movement of my plot" (xv). "The Man Who Lived Underground" also contributed to the setting and theme of *Invisible*

Man: a black man on the run from the police, seeking and finding protection literally underground but also undergoing, in his relationship with others, a complete reversal from conscious irresponsibility and solipsism to a strong commitment to serving and helping them. Ellison's protagonist embodies a similar positive ideal which involves risk but offers both personal integration and reintegration with the community. Dostoevsky's underground man remains in the grips of his neurosis, having cut himself off from human society out of fear and guilt, and refusing to take advantage of his one possible avenue back toward humanity through Lisa. In spite of the legitimacy of his persona's objections to materialist and rationalist thought, Dostoevsky clearly rejects his justifications of inactivity and his wallowing in morbid self-pity. Neither Wright nor Ellison adapts this aspect of psychological impairment to his protagonist, choosing to present a basically sound personality under considerable strain but capable of growth, new identity, and positive action. Ellison's underground man, indulging in flashes of egotism and humor in his extended monologue, resembles Dostoevsky's character more than Wright's does. Both Wright and Ellison develop the idea, found in *The Brothers Karamazov*, of discovering light and life underground, and both approve of their protagonists' decisions to emerge from their isolation.

The Outsider and *Invisible Man*, published only a few months apart, are strikingly alike in their attacks on collectivism and naturalism and in their emphasis on choice, identity, and freedom. Both novels look to *The Devils* somewhat for the portrayal of the radicals' cynicism, their oppression of the individual, and their hypocrisy about helping the masses. Both novels show self-will as a positive drive insofar as it encourages the individual to resist such dehumanizing treatment and to define himself. Both also assert the need for creative choice in the formation of personal identity. But *Invisible Man*, like "The Man Who Lived Underground," lacks the ambivalence of *Native Son* and *The Outsider* on the issue of self-will. Whereas Wright gives qualified approval to Bigger's and Cross's actions, Ellison withholds the heroic tone from his protagonist's project of assertion, implying instead the individual's duty to himself to rise above self-deception to a communal sensitivity.

Ellison's novel reflects his own and Wright's experiences in dealing with the Communist Party. As discussed above, Ellison for a time had strong sympathy for the Party but never formally joined it. The experience of his protagonist thus more clearly resembles that of Wright, who was an official and an active Party member for some eight years and who felt threatened when he attempted to break away. *Invisible Man* presents a protagonist who in spite of his wariness is taken in to some degree by the scientism and materialism of the organization. Cross Damon, in contrast, suspects the ruthlessness of the Party from the start, reflecting Wright's own reluctance to depict his own erroneous inner endorsement of it. Ellison, never having wholly adopted the Party's definition of himself or the world, presumably felt freer to represent such an involvement and subsequent defection.

Invisible Man transcends the protest novel's limitations with its spiritual view of suffering and its insistence on celebration as the heart of life and of art. In contrast to Bigger, Cross, and several of the protagonists from *Uncle Tom's Children*, the Invisible Man is never forced or tempted to kill. Although *The Outsider* does not partake of protest in the manner of *Native Son*, some of Cross's anger (as seen especially in his bashing in the face of the dead white man on the train) can be ascribed to his humiliation by his white boss and presumably by other whites. With the exception of "The Man Who Lived Underground" Wright takes Ivan's skeptical view, that suffering is tragic, absurd, and without meaning. Ellison, consistent with the general view of nineteenth-century Russian writers, believes that suffering can strengthen the spirit, lead to new vision, and prepare one for a rising from the death of a meaningless life. Deutsch summarizes the redemptive power of suffering exhibited in *Invisible Man*: "His suffering does not lead him to despair but to freedom. His suffering, in other words, spiritualizes him" (67). Thus *Invisible Man* does not merely protest against racism and injustice, although it does illuminate certain inequitable and unjust situations. According to Robert Bone, "Ellison perceives, in short, the priestly office of the modern artist and assumes the role of celebrant in his own work. Like the blues singer, he is motivated by an impulse to restore to others a sense of the wholeness of their lives" (26). Ellison himself speaks of the sacred function of the writer as expressing "the wonder of life, in the fullness of which all these outrageous things occur" ("Personality" 8). His sense of the fullness and contrariety of experience allows Ellison to express much more paradox and humor than Wright, resulting in a vision that presents both suffering and joy with greater openness and breadth.

The Invisible Man joins the line of characters including Raskolnikov, Shatov, Kirilov, Stavrogin, Ivan and Dmitry Karamazov, and Fred Daniels, most of whom discover in their individual ways the lie of materialism and/or collectivism, and all of whom find new life in some form of social commitment. As the Invisible Man grows in power in the Brotherhood, he asserts his self-will and interprets freedom as his lack of obligations to anyone. Because he is partly taken in by the organization's materialistic ideology, he attempts to deny the notion of his personal accountability to black people at the same time he is ostensibly working for their benefit. He maintains this contradiction only as long as he can deny the spiritual realities and sources of strength which beckon him throughout the novel to realize his vast possibilities. Ellison uses various forms of folklore and black tradition such as the blues, spirituals, and native idioms to suggest an existential and paradoxical attitude toward suffering, by which the individual celebrates freedom through an ironic and even mocking attitude toward hardship and sorrow. But the Invisible Man's acceptance of these folk forms proceeds very gradually, for at first he is ashamed of them as being only for "low" blacks. He does come to understand, however, that these celebrations of humanity, imperfection, and toughness provide one with strength to endure seemingly hopeless situations. Eventually his conscious integration of these forces into his personality leads him to see the poverty of the Brotherhood's materialist thinking and the cynicism of its exploitation of the individual.

Ellison uses the word "responsibility" quite frequently in *Invisible Man*, stressing it as the corollary of possibility and freedom. He sees the chief significance of his novel as "its experimental attitude and its attempt to return to the mood of personal moral responsibility for democracy which typified the best of our nineteenth-century fiction" (*Shadow* 102). The white men attending the battle royal sneer and laugh at the narrator's use of the phrase "social responsibility" in his speech, allowing it to be spoken but rejecting its application in their society. Ellison, quite aware that he goes beyond the bounds of naturalism and the protest novel, does not judge any racial group or society as a whole, placing primary responsibility on the individual for his own development:

> The hero's invisibility is not a matter of being seen, but a refusal to run the risk of his own humanity, which involves guilt. This is not an attack upon white society! It is what the hero refuses to do in each section which leads to further action. He must assert and achieve his own humanity. (*Shadow* 189)

The protagonist's hibernation in the coal cellar has changed from being a refuge from danger to an outright rejection of responsibility; but as he begins his narration the Invisible Man already hints that he will emerge: "Irresponsibility is part of my invisibility; any way you face it, it is a denial. But to whom can I be responsible, when you refuse to see me? . . . Even the invisible victim is responsible for the fate of all. But I shirked that responsibility" (14). The narrator's dream of the old woman, who says that freedom lies not in hating but in loving, prefigures his eventual growth in this knowledge. The freedom up north of which the black veteran surgeon speaks is not simple civil liberty but a freedom of the personality to develop one's talents and to contribute to society--the same idea that nineteenth-century Russian writers stressed in their attempts to find a place for their superfluous men. The shell-shocked black veterans from the hospital represent the immense challenge posed to the idealistic young black man who aspires to one of the professions. These men have developed psychological disorders because their contributions have been brutally rejected, purely on racial grounds. The brilliant brain surgeon, who was beaten and driven from his profession upon returning to the United States, epitomizes this enforced superfluousness which threatens even those blacks who recognize their social responsibility and attempt to fulfill it.

Ellison's use of folklore in *Invisible Man* parallels the use of native material in early Russian literature, and it contributed to the maturation of black American fiction through encouraging profound acceptance of all aspects of black life. The evolution of Russian "narodnost" or nationalism early in the nineteenth century was assisted by the popularization and assimilation of folklore into the developing literature. The element of self-acceptance inherent in such assimilation helped to develop the confidence in the national psyche necessary for the production of a national as well as a universal literature. Some of the writers of the Harlem Renaissance of the twenties and thirties shied away from the depiction of folk types because many readers, both white and black, objected to images that were thought to reinforce degrading racial stereotypes. The white writer Carl van Vechten depicted black exoticism and primitivism to the point that he was accused of exploiting his material for sensationalistic purposes. With Bigger Thomas Wright certainly does not flinch from representing what he sees as the black man's elemental passion and vengeful reaction against oppression. In *Uncle Tom's Children* the folk nationalism of several characters motivates them even more than their commitment to collectivism as they resist oppression. But Wright's major fiction does not evoke or develop folk traditions to a significant extent, in contrast to *Invisible Man*. In *Shadow and Act* Ellison emphasizes the importance of folklore to Russian literature and to any developing literature: "It's no accident that great literature, the products of individual artists, is erected upon this humble base. The hero of Dostoevsky's *Notes from Underground* and the hero of Gogol's 'The Overcoat' appear in their rudimentary forms far back in Russian folklore'' (*Shadow* 171). Ellison finds that the assimilation of folklore has been important to black people because it "announced the Negro's willingness to trust his own experience, his own sensibilities as to the definition of reality, rather than to allow his masters to define these crucial matters for him'' (Kent 182). Ellison implies that folk art accounts for a large degree of black Americans' self-awareness and endurance, and he recommends that those who wish to understand them should study nineteenth-century Russian writers and learn about black folklore (O'Meally 172). He further insists that the influence of black folk art constitutes an essential part of the American character and identity: "I recognize no American style in literature, in dance, in music, even in assembly-line processes, which does not bear the mark of the American Negro" (McPherson 44).

The clearest gauge of the Invisible Man's growth in knowledge of himself and his world, and of his evolution toward understanding and accepting his freedom, is his changing attitude toward the forms of folk expression which he encounters throughout the novel. Early in the novel he feels ashamed of the poor black citizens near the college, known as the peasants, and of what the officials of the college call their primitive spirituals. Likewise he is deeply embarrassed at Jim Trueblood's ready confession of his unintentional incestuous act with his daughter, which only seems to confirm some of the worst white stereotypes about black people. Yet the narrator's resentment toward Mr. Norton for asking his insensitive questions, and his anger at Trueblood for depicting blacks as passionate primitives, suggests his desire for pride in his people. Trueblood tells the Invisible Man that singing the blues has helped him to come to terms with his guilt and depression and to live with himself. At this point, however, the Invisible Man cannot accept the blues's healing strength, associating them with those folk impulses which supposedly kept black people from advancing in society. Toward Mary Rambo, one of the several other folk figures, he feels both anger at her acceptance of the subservient Sambo image (as symbolized in the bank) and a certain responsibility to repay her kindness and faith in him with a significant contribution to black pride. In spite of his early dislike of spirituals, he keeps hearing the melody of "Swing Low, Sweet Chariot" while listening to the *New World Symphony*.

The electric shock therapy administered at the hospital, symbolic of society's attempt to eradicate personality and identity, becomes a turning point as the Invisible Man finds strength to resist personal effacement in folk memories, sayings, and humor. His new, subtly mocking tone taken in his exit interview with the doctor, echoing the irony and detachment of the black surgeon, marks the beginning of his disillusionment and of the freeing of his personality: "Perhaps I was catching up with myself and had put into words feelings which I had hitherto suppressed" (243). He works for the Brotherhood partly out of selfish desire for acclaim and advancement, but also because of his deepening commitment to black people. His rising disgust with manifestations of black people's negative self-image (e.g., ointments to lighten black skin in order to be "truly beautiful") also indicates his change. His decision to enjoy eating yams on the street, in spite of his earlier embarrassment doing so, becomes a celebration of freedom and of his racial and personal identity. The Invisible Man carries the leg shackle given to him by Brother Tarp, another symbolic folk figure, as a concrete reminder of the very real suffering still inflicted by white people upon blacks. Tod Clifton's Sambo doll represents Clifton's and the Invisible Man's foolishness at being exploited by the Brotherhood. The briefcase which the Invisible Man carries around even through the riot contains the folk symbol of the chain and the symbols of his shattered former selves (the scholarship, the broken Sambo bank with coins, and the Sambo doll) which he now accepts as he prepares to freely choose a new identity for himself. He carries the briefcase through the difficult circumstances because he has undergone a radical change of attitude toward all sorts of folk symbols and sources, from shame and denial to pride.

Throughout *Invisible Man* Ellison presents the dichotomy between the sterility of rationalism and the wisdom and sustenance of black folklore, especially the blues. The black surgeon expresses Ellison's view that the essentials of life are understood by peasants and folk peoples "almost always through experience, though seldom through conscious thought" (89). The vet mocks Norton as a guardian of sterile rationalist thought, "a trustee of consciousness" (88) who "registers with his senses but short-circuits his brain. Nothing has meaning. . . . He's invisible, a walking personification of the Negative; the most perfect achievement of your dreams, sir! The mechanical man" (92). Ellison sounds a paradoxical tone, reminiscent of *Notes from Underground*, as he suggests the primacy of feelings over intellect: "There is an area in which a man's feelings are more rational than his mind, and it is precisely in that area that his will is pulled in several directions at the same time" (560). The blues is the novel's most recurrent folk form, comforting and instructing the Invisible Man and imparting to him some of its ironical perspective. Ellison points out that the existential tradition in black American life proceeds out of the blues and spirituals (Geller 22), and he eloquently summarizes the victory inherent in this tradition:

> The blues is an impulse to keep the painful details and episodes of a brutal experience alive in one's aching consciousness, to finger its jagged grain, and to transcend it, not by the consolation of philosophy but by squeezing from it a near-tragic, near-comic lyricism. . . . Their attraction lies in this, that they at once express both the agony of life and the possibility of conquering it through sheer toughness of spirit. ("Blues" 202, 212)

Much in the spirit of Dostoevsky in *The Devils* and *The Brothers Karamazov*, in *Invisible Man* Ellison asserts that real brotherhood, based on compassion and respect for human personality, must reject all apparent forms of brotherhood which do not respect such values. The Invisible Man becomes involved with the Brotherhood, the materialist, collectivist organization representing the Communist Party (and somewhat like Dostoevsky's vision of the Catholic church in "The Grand Inquisitor") just as he begins to admit the legitimacy of his folk tradition. His first exposure to collectivism, which functions as a sort of warning, occurs when he accidentally enters the union meeting at the Liberty Paint plant, learning first-hand of the members' hostility and disregard for individual rights. He meets members of the Brotherhood ironically just after he decides to eat yams with pride on the street and experiences an intense feeling of freedom in simply being himself. Thus Ellison establishes the opposing forces of individual freedom and authoritarianism vying for his protagonist's sympathies. Because the Invisible Man has left behind, since the electric shock treatment, his former identity as a naive young black man who allowed powerful white and black people to tell him who to be, the Brotherhood attempts to exploit his personal vacuum. His state of tension and ambivalence finds expression after he listens to the mysterious and comical blues of Peter Wheatstraw, unsure whether he feels pride or disgust for black people.

The Invisible Man mistrusts the Brotherhood's authoritarianism, but he represses some of his objections in his effort to acquire personal power and influence in the organization. Just as Dostoevsky does in *The Devils*, and Wright in *The Outsider*, Ellison clearly delineates the collectivist organization's opposition to individual rights and dignity, exemplified in Jack's advice that "you mustn't waste your emotions on individuals, they don't count" (284). The Invisible Man feels a rising respect for poor black people, but Jack seeks to squelch it, focusing on abstract motivations and goals such as duty. Jack tells the narrator that the leaders furnish all ideas, and that the individual must bow to their judgments even if he knows them to be wrong. The members of the Brotherhood pride themselves in their materialism and their rigidly scientific approach to societal problems. The Invisible Man approves of their efforts to control the world and history by science, but he suspects from the beginning that Jack and the Brotherhood only want to use him. In spite of his personal confusion, he decides not to adopt the identity they try to foist upon him but to continue searching for his new self. Still he experiences doubts about the personality he is becoming under the aegis of the organization, as do Shatov and Kirilov in *The Devils*. But the Invisible Man represses what he calls his "dissenting voice" (327), which objects to the Brotherhood's stifling of individuality. Cross, Shatov, and the Invisible Man are all used and victimized by the radicals partly because they assert freedom and personality. The Invisible Man is not killed, but he is exploited by the Brotherhood just when he thinks that he is cleverly using them.

Ellison suggests the inner split of his protagonist (implicit in *The Devils* with the duality and separation of Shatov and Kirilov) by representing his awkward feeling of separation from his body and his rising consciousness that he has two selves in conflict. The Invisible Man's ruthless ambition to use the Brotherhood for his own personal advancement makes understandable the quieting of his conscience or better self. He is called "a petty individualist" (392) by some members of the Brotherhood not for any idealistic support of individual freedom for himself or others but for his thinly disguised ambition. Ironically the Invisible Man himself remains mostly unaware of his egoism and of his infidelity to the Brotherhood's goals and means, taking a tone of sincerely offended innocence when charged with personal ambition, and seeing no contradiction in his resolution to work to the top of the movement. He reaches the nadir of his sensitivity when he blandly echoes the organization's rhetoric in refusing to investigate the meaning of his role in the death of Tod Clifton: "I was no detective, and, politically, individuals were without meaning" (436).

Jack and the Brotherhood cynically exploit the Invisible Man's partial seduction, justifying their murderous betrayal of poor blacks with arguments quite similar to those of the Grand Inquisitor. Jack promises the Invisible Man full freedom within the framework of Brotherhood discipline, knowing that that freedom is illusory and ultimately self-defeating. Jack's exhortations to the committee sound very much like the nihilistic words of Peter Verkhovensky: "We must plan methods of increasing the effectiveness of our agitation, and we must organize the energy that has already been released. . . . Thus it is necessary that we strike immediately and strike hard" (353). The Invisible

Man's self-will blinds him to the Brotherhood's transparent hypocrisy in claiming a policy of nonviolence while actually planning riots and deaths of black people. The leaders of the movement attempt to justify withdrawing their support of black people and the subsequent violence as required by "scientific necessity" (492). In several statements, Jack and the Brotherhood sound much like the Grand Inquisitor in their contempt for most people's intelligence and ability to bear the burden of freedom. Therefore they posit an intellectual elite who rule the masses by removing their powers of choice:

> It's impossible not to take advantage of the people. . . . The trick
> is to take advantage of them in their own best interest. . . . Would
> you like to resurrect God to take responsibility? No, brother, we
> have to make such decisions ourselves. Even if we must some-
> times appear as charlatans. (493, 494)

Ellison refutes this view with observations, similar to those in *Notes from Underground*, on the stubborn primacy of irrational human will and whim over rational authoritarian control or even rational self-advantage. Thus the blacks' setting fire to their own tenement apartment building becomes a perverse act but a free one, a celebration of their power over some portion of their lives. Ellison, like Wright and Dostoevsky, observes that there are positive aspects of self-assertion even when it has self-destructive consequences. The Invisible Man feels a sense of exaltation in the sense that these people "carried it through alone; the decision their own, and their own action. Capable of their own action" (536).

The Invisible Man is taken in by the Brotherhood's offers of vanity and power, but at the same time he does manage to grow gradually in individuality through his choice of a new self. After the pivotal incident of his recovery from electric shock through folk associations, another important development takes place during his first speech for the Brotherhood. In spite of his training in the effacement of personality, he reverts to techniques learned back home, confides his subjective feelings to his audience, and proclaims that he is becoming more human. Naturally the Brotherhood objects that his is the antithesis of the scientific approach. But the Invisible Man suddenly has seen his personal boundaries disappear in a dizzying array of possibilities. He now understands and endorses the words of a former teacher of his, that "our task is that of making ourselves individuals. The conscience of a race is the gift of its individuals who see, evaluate, record. . . . We create the race by creating ourselves" (346). He breaks finally with the self which he had partially accepted from the Brotherhood when he suspects that he may have had some responsibility in the death of Tod Clifton. After he does recognize his unwitting complicity in the deaths of Clifton and those killed in the riot, he commits himself to undermining and defeating all those such as Jack, Emerson, Norton, and Bledsoe, who manipulate others and keep them from realizing their freedom.

Similar to *Notes from Underground* and *The Brothers Karamazov* as well as to "The Man Who Lived Underground" and *The Outsider*, *Invisible Man* works the theme of going underground and dying to an old self as a means of rising to a new existence. Images of the underground include the darkened boxing ring, the basement of the paint factory, the subway, the platform in the pit of the coliseum where he delivers his first speech, the darkened world he observes through his sunglasses as Rinehart, and the coal bin where he takes refuge from the chaos above. With the aged black man laboring three levels beneath the ground at the Liberty Paint Company, Ellison implies the contribution black people have made to everything American but also their lack of recognition or reward. The Invisible Man nearly dies in the explosion due to his fight with the old man; he rises from the underground only to face the torment of electric shock. Ellison has the Invisible Man enter the subway at several critical junctures to suggest the end or loss of another phase of false identity. He takes the subway after the shock treatment has failed to wipe out his personality and just before he meets Mary Rambo; he also goes underground after Tod's murder, as he seeks to understand why he died. Ellison shows that these "deaths" can be transformed into births and can strengthen the individual, provided he chooses freedom and self-knowledge. As part of the Invisible Man's personal investigation of his role in Tod's death, he dons his Rinehart disguise, goes metaphorically underground, and discovers more than ever that fluidity and possibility are ever-present. His final movement underground, into the coal bin, becomes his most dramatic and makes possible his most profound transformation. While underground he becomes as absolutely free as Fred Daniels--free of all external needs and threats. Yet both men experience the sterility and failure of solipsistic self-assertion. Ellison comments in *Shadow and Act* that the Invisible Man's "movement vertically downward, (not into a 'sewer,' Freud notwithstanding, but into a coal cellar, a source of heat, light, power, and, through association with the character's motivation, self-perception) is a process of rising to an understanding of his human condition" (57). The Invisible Man finds a first source of light underground in burning the symbols and insignia of the false identities he has accepted from others: his high school diploma, Clifton's doll, the anonymous letter of warning about the Brotherhood, and the slip with his Brotherhood name. Ellison echoes the idea of the pre-Civil War underground railroad as a passage to freedom with his reference to "a section of the basement that was shut off and forgotten during the nineteenth century" (5). With this phrase he also connects his novel with the nineteenth-century American tradition of moral concern which Ellison finds so important in the work of Melville and Twain.

The Invisible Man's gradual discovery of the primacy of individual dignity guides him toward his personal philosophy of social responsibility, which he deduces during his hibernation underground. Bledsoe mocks his idealistic, supposedly naive notions about dignity, advising him to acquire and use power instead. Ellison shows his protagonist's unconscious search for dignity hampered by both white and black people who abandon their personalistic folk traditions in favor of selfish attainment. Tod Clifton takes to selling Sambo dolls on the street as a public, if bizarre act of repentance for his unknowing complicity in the betrayal of freedom by the Brotherhood. His death occurs when his assertion of dignity is met with murderous force by the policeman. In the subway the Invisible Man observes the symbolic funeral ceremony for Tod by the handsome, agile young black men who seem superfluous to the white world but who are "the saviors, the true leaders, the bearers of something precious" (431). This meditation on shared human potential inspires the Invisible Man to organize a public funeral for Tod, despite certain opposition by the Brotherhood, "both as a means of avenging him and of preventing other such deaths" (437). The funeral becomes a mass demonstration of black pride which fills the Invisible Man with "transcendent emotion" as he realizes "that I was listening to something within myself" (442). The rioters' destruction of their own apartment buildings, which clearly goes against their own interest, demonstrates to him that human dignity is more important than material advantage, a theme especially evident in *Notes from Underground*.

The several rebirths the Invisible Man experiences in the novel culminate in his recognition of personal responsibility not just for the people killed in the riots, but for all people--another echo of Dmitry Karamazov and Fred Daniels. After the murder of Clifton, the Invisible Man begins to suspect his own culpability: "Although I knew no man could do much about it, I felt responsible. . . . And it was all my fault. . . . I'd been asleep, dreaming" (433). Ellison uses the word "responsibility" as a motif, an echo which grows in strength the more his protagonist meditates on it. The Invisible Man tells Jack that he organized the funeral based on his personal responsibility, a concept completely inimical to Brotherhood ideology. After his absurd sexual encounter with Sybil, he grapples with his conscience over allowing her to degrade herself, and he tries to excuse himself: "My action, my--the painful word formed as disconnectedly as her wobbly smile--my *responsibility*? All of it? I'm invisible" (514). The Invisible Man admires Rinehart's fluidity, but he rejects his inconsistency and irresponsibility, calling it "Rinehartism--cynicism" (493).

Similar to Shatov when he rejects the radicals for their diabolical actions in *The Devils*, the Invisible Man finally realizes that the Brotherhood has used him to bring about rioting and death in the ghetto, and that his pursuit of false, selfish freedom has made this possible: "By pretending to agree I *had* agreed, had made myself responsible for that huddled form lighted by flame and gunfire in the street, and all the others whom now the night was making ripe for death" (541). As he reflects on his grandfather's deathbed advice, he concludes that it implies not chaos but conscientious concern on the part of each individual for all others: "Did he mean that we had to take the responsibility for all of it, for the men as well as the principle, because we were the heirs who must use the principle because no other fitted our needs?" (561). Ellison couples a rejection of environmental determinism with an assertion of the individual's responsibility to look within himself:

> The fact is that you carry part of your sickness within you, at least I do as an invisible man. I carried my sickness and though for a long time I tried to place it in the outside world, the attempt to write it down shows me that at least half of it lay within me. Deep down you come to suspect that you're yourself to blame. *That* is the real soul-sickness, the spear in the side. (562)

Ellison also uses the word "possibility" quite frequently, especially near the end of the novel as a positive side-effect of individual responsibility and as an invitation for the individual to take creative control over his life. As soon as the Invisible Man abandons his Brotherhood identity, which was rigidly curtailed by authoritarian boundaries, he discovers that he is more free than he has ever dreamed. Having rejected the materialist negation of personality and freedom, he finds that, all boundaries down, "freedom was not only the recognition of necessity, it was the recognition of possibility" (488). He also recognizes that unlimited self-will has led to the destruction of others and nearly of himself. He does not approve of Rinehart's running numbers or his pimping, but the Invisible Man sees him as a symbol of possibility itself and as a man who somewhat heroically accepts the complexities and challenges of individual, existential freedom. The Invisible Man sums up his own growth in accepting freedom in a passage which also epitomizes Ellison's positive alternative to naturalism:

> I started out with my share of optimism. I believed in hard work and progress and action, but now, after first being "for" society and then "against" it, I assign myself no rank or any limit, and such an attitude is very much against the trend of the times. But my world has become one of infinite possibilities. What a phrase-- still it's a good phrase and a good view of life, and a man shouldn't accept any other; that much I've learned underground. Until some gang succeeds in putting this world in a strait jacket, its definition is possibility. (563)

With the conclusion of *Invisible Man* Ellison sounds an ecstatic affirmation of survival, resurrection, and social responsibility which echoes and rivals that of "The Man Who Lived Underground" and *The Brothers Karamazov*. However, some critics object rather strenuously to the novel's ending. Marcus Klein, for example, finds that "the novel doesn't finally go anywhere. It is a fault that apparently led Ellison to the desperate, empty, and programmatic optimism of the last few pages of the novel" (76). Leonard Deutsch, however, argues quite thoroughly and convincingly that the whole novel develops and prepares for this affirmative vision, which is "inherent in the book's textures and structure, in its jazz modulations and the development of its spiritual epiphanies" (146). The protagonist's psychologically credible and carefully evolved creed of social responsibility takes concrete form before his final descent underground, as seen in his willingness to sacrifice his life for others' advancement in self-knowledge. Thus his final point of view parallels that of Shatov, Dmitry and Ivan Karamazov, and Fred Daniels. The Invisible Man declares, explicitly and simply, his wish that all people aboveground would "stop running and respect and love one another" (548). He chose his temporary life underground primarily as a means of survival. But he concludes that he needs the world above as the natural element of his freedom, as the context in which he can be responsible to others, as the only place where he can fulfill himself through loving.

Unlike the narrator of *Notes from Underground*, who remains stalled in his neurosis, the Invisible Man unifies his personality by choosing to accept the weight of freedom and the lightness of possibility. At the novel's conclusion he resolves, as does Fred Daniels, to rise to the world above in order to play his "socially responsible role" (568). He takes the same risk as Daniels in returning to a hostile, threatening environment, but we sense that his fate will be much more positive. Just as Dmitry Karamazov accepts his escape and exile to the spiritually dead America, Daniels and the Invisible Man return to the spiritual underground of the world above. All three protagonists, however, acquire a happiness and peace of mind which make them new men.

Conclusion

Dostoevsky, Wright, and Ellison all struggled with the role of creative revolt in the dichotomy of self versus community. Each writer's early work and life reflects a degree of involvement with radicalism and naturalism which would later be reversed by his evolving understanding of the primacy of individual freedom and the tendency of those ideologies to contradict freedom. The fiction of each writer deepens from early social analysis with naturalistic implications to more complex, paradoxical examinations of personality and identity. All three acknowledge first, that the human personality will assert itself, sometimes even in the most repressive circumstances, and even if that assertion causes further suffering to oneself. Second, they observe that this apparently universal need for rebellion can benefit the individual who comes to realize his freedom and autonomy, but that the person's failure to discover limits to self-assertion can result in solipsism, nihilism, and self-destruction. The person living by self-will often presumes to have attained the height of creativity, for he may feel that he has gone beyond conventional morality, to lonelier but more exalted territory. Third, these writers show (although Wright does so with some ambivalence) the slavery of apparently ultimate freedom, and the higher creativity of revolt which transcends self-will. The discovery of one's freely chosen social contribution makes one's individuality more striking and fulfilling, as the dichotomy between self and community disappears. Like Shatov, Ivan and Dmitry Karamazov, Fred Daniels, and the Invisible Man, the individual who finds happiness in surrendering self-will feels relieved of a freedom that has become hollow, rootless, and burdensome. He exchanges it for a lighter burden of freedom whose values are social connection and responsibility. The realm and consciousness of the transformed individual remain somewhat mysterious and inexplicable. But he is marked by his

186

passionate faith in communication, action, and affirmation.

Both nineteenth-century Russian fiction and twentieth-century black American fiction deal explicitly with the individual's self-definition over against societal interferences and also his need to reintegrate himself in some meaningful way with others. Both literatures reflect on the regeneration of the individual as the key to the deliverance and salvation of a people. Whereas Dostoevsky and his contemporaries were almost obsessed with ideas of individual moral betterment and the construction of a more just social order, the dominant white culture in America too often turns away from individual self-examination and avoids the introspection necessary for deep and lasting social change. According to Baldwin,

> The importance of writers in this country is this, that this country is yet to be discovered in any real sense. . . . I suspect that there is something much more important and much more real which produces the Cadillacs, the refrigerator, and the atom bomb, and what produces it, after all, is something which we don't seem to want to look at, and *that is the person*. (*Nobody* 153-54)

The return to profound moral searching in twentieth-century American literature is not exclusive to black literature, but, as Ellison suggests, that searching does seem to be endemic in the quest of black writers, who must puzzle out the keys to survival in a frequently hostile or indifferent white society. Baldwin associates the question of America's survival with its treatment of black Americans: "The price of the transformation of America is the unconditional freedom of the Negro; it is not too much to say that he who has been so long rejected must now be embraced, and at no matter what psychic or social risk" (*Fire* 108).

One might trace nineteenth-century Russian fiction's theme of the superfluous man through black American fiction of the twentieth century, noting the frequently societally enforced superfluousness of black people which, even when certain societal restrictions are removed, can devolve into nihilistic self-assertion, as with Bigger Thomas and Cross Damon. Ellison offers a brighter vision than Wright of the "useful" or "new" black American, who can learn to accept his weaknesses and to explore and develop his strengths through fidelity to his particular folk culture. Gogol identifies the typically Russian attitude toward suffering, shared especially by Wright in "The Man Who Lived Underground" and Ellison in *Invisible Man*, which accentuates social responsibility and compassion: "It is by suffering and grief that we are destined to procure some grains of a wisdom impossible to acquire from books. But whoever has acquired one of these crumbs has not the right to conceal it from others" (*Passages* 91). Vyacheslav Ivanov's mystical view of suffering, inspired by Dostoevsky, holds that even apparently meaningless suffering, experienced in the depths of despair, can help to heal oneself and others:

> The sacramental significance, and thus the justification of suffering, resides in the fact that the victim, without knowing that he does so, suffers not only for himself, but also for others; that he not only himself experiences salvation through suffering, but also, whether he knows it or not, is saving others. (81)

This sacramental character of the suffering of the protagonists in the works of Dostoevsky, Wright, and Ellison links these characters with each other and with all others even when they defiantly separate themselves from all humanity.

Selected Bibliography

Works by Wright, Ellison, and Dostoevsky

Dostoevsky, Fyodor. *The Brothers Karamazov*. Ed. Ralph E. Matlaw. Trans. Constance Garnett. New York: Norton, 1976.

---. *Crime and Punishment*. Ed. George Gibian. Trans. Jesse Coulson. 2nd ed. New York: Norton, 1975.

---. *The Devils*. Trans. David Magarshack. Middlesex, England: Penguin, 1971.

---. *Dostoevsky: Letters and Reminiscences*. Trans. S. Koteliansky and J. Murry. New York: Knopf, 1923.

---. "Dostoevsky's Letters." *The Brothers Karamazov*. By Dostoevsky. Ed. Ralph E. Matlaw. Trans. Constance Garnett. New York: Norton, 1976. 751-69.

---. "Dostoevsky's Letters." *Crime and Punishment*. By Dostoevsky. Ed. George Gibian. Trans. Jesse Coulson. 2nd ed. New York: 1975. 476-80.

---. "Dostoevsky's Notebooks." *The Brothers Karamazov*. By Dostoevsky. Ed. Ralph E. Matlaw. Trans. Constance Garnett. New York: Norton, 1976. 769-70.

---. "Dostoevsky's Notebooks." *Crime and Punishment*. By Dostoevsky. Ed. George Gibian. Trans. Jesse Coulson. 2nd ed. New York: Norton, 1975. 470-76.

---. *The Double. Great Short Works of Dostoevsky*. Trans. George Bird. New York: Harper and Row, 1968.

---. *The House of the Dead*. Trans. Constance Garnett. New York: MacMillan, 1959.

---. *The Idiot*. Trans. David Magarshack. Baltimore: Penguin, 1955.

---. *The Notebooks for Crime and Punishment*. Ed., trans. Edward Wasiolek. Chicago: Univ. of Chicago Press, 1967.

---. *The Notebooks for The Possessed*. Ed. Edward Wasiolek. Trans. Victor Terras. Chicago: Univ. of Chicago Press, 1968.

---. *Notes from Underground*. Trans. Andrew MacAndrew. New York: New American Library, 1961.

---. *Poor People and a Little Hero*. Trans. David Magarshack. Garden City, NJ: Doubleday, 1968.

---. *Winter Notes on Summer Impressions*. Trans. Richard Renfield. New York: McGraw-Hill, 1955.

Ellison, Ralph. "Afternoon." *American Writing*. Ed. Hans Otto Storm et. al. Prairie City, IL: J. A. Decker, 1940. 28-37.

---. "The Art of Fiction: an Interview." Gottesman, *Merill Studies* 38-49.

---. "The Birthmark." *New Masses* 36, No. 2 (1940): 16-17.

---. "A Completion of Personality: an Interview." Hersey, *Critical Essays* 7-24.

---. "Flying Home." *Cross Section*. Ed. Edwin Seaver. New York: L. B. Fischer, 1944. 469-85.

---. Going to the Territory. New York: Random House, 1986.

---. "Indivisible Man: an Interview." *The Atlantic* 226, No. 6 (1970): 45-60.

---. Introduction. *Invisible Man*. New York: Vintage Books, 1972. v-xx.

190

---. *Invisible Man*. New York: Vintage Books, 1972.

---. "King of the Bingo Game." *Tomorrow* 4, No. 2 (1944): 29-33.

---. "Mister Toussan." *New Masses* 41, No. 5 (1941): 19-20.

---. "Recent Negro Fiction." *New Masses* 40, No. 6 (1941): 22-26.

---. "Richard Wright and Negro Fiction." *Direction* 4, No. 5 (1941): 12-13.

---. "Richard Wright's Blues." Hakutani, *Critical Essays* 201-12.

---. *Shadow and Act*. London: Secker and Warburg, 1964.

---. "Slick Gonna Learn." *Direction* 2, No. 5 (1939): 10-16.

---. "Society, Morals, and the Novel." *The Living Novel: a Symposium*. Ed. Granville Hicks. New York: MacMillan, 1957. 71-94.

---. "That I Had the Wings." *Common Ground* 3, No. 4 (1943): 30-37.

---. "A Very Stern Discipline." *Harper's* 234 (1967): 76-95.

Wright, Richard. *American Hunger*. New York: Harper and Row, 1977.

---. *Black Boy*. New York: Harper and Row, 1945.

---. "Blueprint for Negro Writing." *Richard Wright Reader*. Eds. Ellen Wright and Michel Fabre. New York: Harper and Row, 1978. 36-49.

---. Introduction. *Native Son*. By Wright. New York: Harper and Row, 1940. vii-xxxiv.

---. "The Man Who Lived Underground." *Richard Wright Reader*. Eds. Ellen Wright and Michel Fabre. New York: Harper and Row, 1978. 517-76.

---. *Native Son*. New York: Harper and Row, 1940.

---. *The Outsider*. New York: Harper and Row, 1953.

---. *Uncle Tom's Children*. New York: Harper and Row, 1936.

Works by Others: Books

Aaron, Daniel. *Writers on the Left: Episodes in American Literary Communism*. New York: Harcourt, Brace, and World, 1961.

Baldwin, James. *The Fire Next Time*. New York: Dial Press, 1963.

---. *Nobody Knows My Name*. New York: Dell, 1961.

---. *Notes of a Native Son*. Boston: Beacon Press, 1955.

Berdyaev, Nikolai. *Dostoevsky*. Trans. Donald Attwater. New York: Meridian Books, 1957.

---. *The Russian Idea*. New York: MacMillan, 1948.

Brignano, Russell C. *Richard Wright: an Introduction to the Man and His Works*. Pittsburgh: Univ. of Pittsburgh Press, 1970.

Browne, Claude. *Manchild in the Promised Land*. New York: New American Library, 1965.

Cerny, Vaclav. *Dostoevsky and His Devils*. Trans. F. Galan. Ann Arbor: Ardis, 1975.

Chernyshevsky, Nikolai. *What Is to Be Done?* Trans. Benjamin Tucker. New York: Vintage Books, 1961.

Deutsch, Leonard. "Affirmation in the Work of Ralph Ellison." Diss. Kent State Univ. 1972.

Dowler, Wayne. *Dostoevsky, Grigoryev, and Native Soil Conservatism*. Toronto: Univ. of Toronto Press, 1982.

Fabre, Michel. *The Unfinished Quest of Richard Wright*. Trans. Isabel Barzun. New York: William Morrow, 1973.

Foner, Philip S. *American Socialism and Black Americans*. Westport, CT: Greenwood Press, 1977.

Foner, Philip S. and James S. Allen, eds. *American Communism and Black Americans: a Documentary History, 1919-1929*. Philadelphia: Temple Univ. Press, 1987.

Frank, Joseph. *Dostoevsky: the Seeds of Revolt, 1821-1849*. Princeton, NJ: Princeton Univ. Press, 1976.

---. *Dostoevsky: the Stir of Liberation, 1860-1865*. Princeton, NJ: Princeton Univ. Press, 1986.

---. *Dostoevsky: the Years of Ordeal, 1850-1859*. Princeton, NJ: Princeton Univ. Press, 1983.

Gogol, Nikolai. *Diary of a Madman and Other Stories*. Trans. Andrew MacAndrew. New York: New American Library, 1960.

---. *Selected Passages from Correspondence with Friends*. Trans. Jesse Zeldin. Nashville: Vanderbilt Univ. Press, 1969.

Gottesman, Ronald, comp. *The Merill Studies in Invisible Man*. Columbus, Ohio: Merill, 1971.

Hakutani, Yoshinobu, ed. *Critical Essays on Richard Wright*. Boston: G. K. Hall, 1982.

Hersey, John, ed. *Ralph Ellison: a Collection of Critical Essays*. Englewood, NJ: Prentice-Hall, 1974.

Herzen, Alexander. *From the Other Shore and The Russian People and Socialism*. Trans. Moura Budberg. London: Weidenfeld and Nicolson, 1956.

Hill, Herbert, ed. *Soon, One Morning: New Writing by American Negroes, 1940-62*. New York: Knopf, 1969.

Hingley, Ronald. *Nihilists*. New York: Delacorte Press, 1967.

Howard, June. *Form and History in American Literary Naturalism*. Chapel Hill: Univ. of North Carolina, 1985.

Ivanov, Vyacheslav. *Freedom and the Tragic Life: a Study in Dostoevsky*. Trans. Norman Cameron. New York: Noonday Press, 1957.

Jackson, Robert Louis. *The Art of Dostoevsky*. Princeton, NJ: Princeton Univ. Press, 1981.

---. *Dostoevsky's Underground Man in Russian Literature*. The Hague, Netherlands: Mouton, 1958.

Kierkegaard, Soren. *Either/Or*. Trans. David F. Swenson. Garden City, NY: Doubleday, 1959.

---. *Works of Love*. Trans. Howard and Edna Hong. New York: Harper and Row, 1962.

Kinnamon, Keneth. *The Emergence of Richard Wright*. Urbana: Univ. of Illinois Press, 1972.

List, Robert. *The Joyce-Ellison Connection*. Washington, D. C.: Univ Press of America, 1982.

Lowrie, Donald. *Religious Prophet: Life of Berdyaev*. New York: Harper and Brothers, 1960.

Malia, Martin. *Alexander Herzen and the Birth of Russian Socialism*. Cambridge: Harvard Univ. Press, 1961.

Margolies, Edward. *The Art of Richard Wright*. Carbondale: Southern Illinois Press, 1969.

Mathewson, Rufus. *The Positive Hero in Russian Literature*. Stanford, CA: Stanford Univ. Press, 1975.

Matlaw, Ralph E., ed. *Belinsky, Chernyshevsky, and Dobrolyubov: Selected Criticism*. New York: E. P. Dutton, 1962.

Maurina, Zenta. *Dostoevsky: Prophet of a Soul*. Trans. C. P. Finlayson. London: James Clarke, n.d.

O'Meally, Robert. *The Craft of Ralph Ellison*. Cambridge: Harvard Univ. Press, 1980.

Pizer, Donald. *Twentieth Century American Literary Naturalism: an Interpretation*. Carbondale: Southern Illinois Univ. Press, 1982.

Ray, David, and Robert Farnsworth, eds. *Richard Wright: Impressions and Perspectives*. Ann Arbor: Univ. of Michigan Press, 1971.

Reilly, John. *Twentieth Century Interpretations of Invisible Man*. Englewood Cliffs, NJ: Prentice-Hall, 1970.

Rudwick, Elliott. *W. E. B. DuBois: a Study in Minority Group Leadership*. Philadelphia: Univ. of

Pennsylvania Press, 1960.

Solovyov, Vladimir. *Solovyov on Godmanhood.* Trans. Peter Zouboff. Poughkeepsie, NY: Harmon Printing House, 1944.

Terras, Victor. *A Karamazov Companion.* Madison: Univ. of Wisconsin Press, 1981.

Walcutt, Charles Child. *American Literary Naturalism: a Divided Stream.* Minneapolis: Univ. of Minnesota Press, 1956.

Williams, William Carlos. *In the American Grain.* New York: New Directions, 1956.

Works by Others: Articles

Belinsky, Vissarion. "Letter to N. V. Gogol." Matlaw, *Belinsky* 83-92.

Bem, Alexander. "The Problem of Guilt in Dostoevsky's Fiction." *Crime and Punishment.* By Dostoevsky. Ed. George Gibian. Trans. Jesse Coulson. 2nd ed. New York: Norton, 1975. 626-29.

Berdyaev, Nikolai. "Dostoevsky, the Nature of Man, and Evil." *Crime and Punishment.* By Dostoevsky. Ed. George Gibian. Trans. Jesse Coulson. 2nd ed. New York: Norton, 1975. 571-77.

Berlin, Isaiah. Introduction. *From the Other Shore and The Russian People and Socialism.* By Alexander Herzen. Trans. Moura Budberg. London: Weidenfeld and Nicolson, 1956. vii-xxiii.

Bone, Robert. "Ralph Ellison and the Uses of the Imagination." Reilly, *Interpretations* 18-34.

Chernyshevsky, Nikolai. "The Russian at the Rendez-vous." Matlaw, *Belinsky* 108-29.

Dobrolyubov, Nikolai. "When Will the Real Day Come?" Matlaw, *Belinsky* 176-226.

Fabre, Michel. Introduction. *Richard Wright Reader.* Eds. Ellen Wright and Michel Fabre. New York: Harper and Row, 1978. vii-xxiv.

Frank, Joseph. "The World of Raskolnikov." *Crime and Punishment.* By Dostoevsky. Ed. George Gibian. Trans. Jesse Coulson. 2nd ed. New York: Norton, 1975. 560-71.

Geller, Allen. "An Interview with Ralph Ellison." *Tamarack Review* 32 (1964): 3-24.

Gibian, George. "Traditional Symbolism in *Crime and Punishment.*" *Crime and Punishment.* By Dostoevsky. Ed. George Gibian. Trans. Jesse Coulson. 2nd ed. New York: Norton, 1975. 519-36.

Kent, George. "Ralph Ellison and Afro-American Folk and Cultural Tradition." Hersey, *Critical Essays* 174-85.

Klein, Marcus. "Ralph Ellison's *Invisible Man.*" Gottesman, *Merill Studies* 62-90.

Lawrence, D. H. "The Grand Inquisitor." *The Brothers Karamazov.* By Dostoevsky. Ed. Ralph E. Matlaw. Trans. Constance Garnett. New York: Norton, 1976. 829-36.

Magarshack, David. Introduction. *The Devils.* Trans. David Magarshack. Middlesex, England: Penguin, 1971. vii-xvii.

Magistrale, Tony. "From St. Petersburg to Chicago: Wright's *Crime and Punishment.*" *Comparative Literature Studies* 23 (1986): 59-69.

McPherson, James Alan. "Indivisible Man." Hersey, *Critical Essays* 39-55.

Neal, Larry. "Ellison's Zoot Suit." Hersey, *Critical Essays* 54-67.

Nisula, Dasha Culic. "Dostoevsky and Richard Wright: From St. Petersburg to Chicago." *Dostoevsky and the Human Condition After a Century.* Eds. Alexej Ugrinsky, Frank Lambasa, and Valija Ozolin. New York: Greenwood Press, 1986. 163-70.

Stanton, Robert. "Outrageous Fiction: *Crime and Punishment, The Assistant*, and *Native Son.*" *Pacific Coast Philology* 4 (1969): 52-58.

Index

194

Lawd Today, 10, 56
Lawrence, D. H., 153, 157
Lenin, Vladimir, 46
List, Robert, 43
Lowrie, Donald, 21, 22, 136, 138

Magarshack, David, 138, 139
Magistrale, Tony, 77
Maikov, Apollon, 25, 28
Malia, Martin, 11, 12, 13, 15, 19
Malraux, Andre, 75
"Man Who Lived Underground, The," 4, 7, 8, 37, 94, 107, 133, 134, 135, 156, 161-166, 167, 183
Margolies, Edward, 57, 59, 60, 94, 103, 107, 113, 161
Marxism, 3, 21, 49, 53, 55
materialism, 4, 9, 13, 15, 18, 24, 38, 82, 83, 88, 141, 182
Mathewson, Rufus, 11, 15, 17, 18
Matlaw, Ralph, 18
McKay, Claude, 47
McPherson, James, 173
Muller, Johannes, 12

native soil movement, 19, 20
Native Son, 4, 5, 6, 7, 8, 34, 43, 54, 56, 77, 78, 79, 91, 92, 94-107, 120
naturalism, 6, 7, 54, 55, 74, 92, 96, 124, 183
Neal, Larry, 44, 63, 66
Netochka Nezvanova, 29
Nisula, Dasha Culic, 77
Notes from Underground, 4, 5, 10, 32, 37, 38, 41, 42, 74, 87, 133, 167, 168, 172, 175, 178, 179, 181, 184
Novalis, 12

Ogaryov, Nikolai, 12
O'Meally, Robert, 42, 44, 66, 67, 68, 69, 71, 97
The Outsider, 4, 5, 6, 7, 8, 34, 56, 73, 77-80, 91, 92, 94, 100, 101, 106, 107, 108-131, 157, 168

Padmore, George, 63
Petrashevsky group, 14, 23, 28
Pisarev, Dmitry, 15, 16, 18
Pizer, Donald, 54
pochvenniki, men of the soil, 19, 20
Poor Folk, 9, 23, 25, 26, 43
Pushkin, Alexander, 2, 3,

Ray, David, 50, 107
Rudwick, Elliott, 47, 48

Saint-Simon, Comte de, 32
Sand, George, 32
Schelling, Friedrich, 11, 12, 24
Schiller, Johann, 12, 14, 24
Shadow and Act, 44, 64, 70, 71, 72, 73, 74, 75, 97, 171, 172, 173, 180
socialism: Russian, 4, 8, 10, 21, 28-32, 36-38, 151; Christian, 18, 19, 24-25, 30; Utopian, 25, 28, 80, 81, 87, 88; American, 45-46
Socialist Party, 46, 48
Solovyov, Vladimir, 3, 21, 94
Sprandel, Katherine, 106
superfluous man, theme of, 2, 7, 16, 18, 68, 129, 137, 171-172

Toomer, Jean, 2
Turgenev, Ivan, 16
Twain, Mark, 74

Uncle Tom's Children, 6, 10, 55, 98, 101, 103
Utilitarianism, 18, 38, 39, 81-82

Van Vechten, Carl, 172

Walcutt, Charles, 55
Washington, Booker T., 47
Winter Notes on Summer Impressions, 10, 32, 36, 41

Zola, Emile, 54, 95

Chester M. Hedgepeth

THEORIES OF SOCIAL ACTION IN BLACK LITERATURE

American University Studies: Series XIX (General Literature). Vol. 2
ISBN 0-8204-0311-3   VII, 158 pages.   hardcover US $ 29.60

Recommended price – alterations reserved

Theories of Social Action in Black Literature is a comparative analysis of exemplary literature that conveys the religious and secular basis of social action among Blacks during the first half of the twentieth century. The study compares and contrasts the themes of hopelessness and despair in the works of selected black novelists with the more optimistic tone of the leaders of social action movements. In the case of the novelists, the purpose is to show from an analysis of prototypical tragic literature the prominence of physical and spiritual suffering that results from the *deus absconditus* of Old Testament and selected black fiction. In particular, this section focuses on the «Samson Syndrome» as the historical and religious representation of negative self-assertion that has as its intent the transformation of a culturally repressive society.

The activists serve both individually and collectively to gain freedom. Their actions may be characterized as transcending, transforming, or accommodating. The aim of the analysis of both individual and collective leadersphip styles is to show the contrast in means and goals between the artists and the activists.

Contents: This study is a comparative analysis of exemplary literature that conveys the religious and secular basis of social action among Blacks during the first half of the twentieth century.

PETER LANG PUBLISHING, INC.
62 West 45th Street
USA – New York, NY 10036